I0776770

DEMOCRACY SNAPSHOTS

- Carlos Alberto Montaner
- Armando Valladares
- Carlos Sanchez Berzain
- Beatriz E. Rangel
- Luis Fleischman
- Cesar Vidal

THE DEMOCRACY PAPER
No. 13

ISBN:1979044635

Design: Kiko Arocha
www.alexlib.com

Fondo Editorial
Interamercian Institute for Democracy
2100 Coral Way. Ste. 500
Miami, FL 33145
U.S.A.
Tel: (786) 409-4554
Fax: (786) 409-4576
www.intdemocratic.org
iid@intdemocratic.org

INDEX

FOREWORD

By James E. Keeble

The Interamerican Institute for Democracy (IID) is a nonpartisan, nonprofit organization, established more than ten years ago. It is made up of political experts, former government officials, lawyers, journalists, scholars, businessmen and women of diverse backgrounds and nationalities, united in the common cause of promoting liberty, democracy and defending human rights, within a frame of pluralism and tolerance.

The IID is a leading research and advocacy organization known for its accurate seminars, round tables, conferences, forums, academic research, effective use of media and publications, often in partnership with local organizations and other academic institutions. Its editorial fund has edited and published more than fifty publications in English and Spanish.

Each year, the IID publishes a report and organizes at least one Forum at US Congress in Washington, DC; where important scholars and world influential leaders are invited to discuss and brief on democratic conditions in the Americas, generating extensive coverage in local and regional media. As part of its programs, the IID publishes "The Democracy Papers", which contain studies on the progress or decline of democracy and provides information on the social-political situation of the region. Its activities focus on integrating the academic aspects of political science with pragmatic politics. This combination has resulted in a more realistic approach and a more effective use of political activism.

Within this framework, the IID Directors have contributed to this issue of "The Democracy Papers", with several essays focused on essential elements of democracy, to enshrine the "respect for human rights and fundamental freedoms," the "exercise of power in accordance with the rule of law", and the "separation of powers and independence of branches of government" which are -among the others recognized in The Inter-American Democratic Charter. The absence of those elements makes democracy non-existent, and gives rise to authoritarianism and dictatorship.

The essay "The Anatomy of Racism" by Carlos Alberto Montaner centers on a tweet by Representative King. Explaining how Racism is a feature inherent to human nature. Children are born without it until they gradually acquire an identity. Then he moves forward to talk about Nationalism and sports fanaticism, closing his analysis with the fact that "25 centuries ago in Athens, Zeno the Stoic dared to say that people had rights beyond parentage and place of birth". This essay is an important contribution to this Democracy Paper because it carefully presents answers to implicit questions in this discussion and constitutes an extensive venture in the field of tolerance and intellectual circumstances.

"Human Rights in Cuba" is an essay written by former U.S. Ambassador to the United Nations -Commission on Human Rights- Armando Valladares. It is about the situation of Human Rights on the Island. The main starting point of this essay is that a one-sixth of the Cuban population lives abroad (in exile). Later he develops his work on Human Rights conditions on the island, which are based on irrefutable facts. First, Cuba is the longest dictatorships of this continent, and second, the tyrant Fidel Castro has always lied. This work is a summary of material facts by someone who has dedicated his life to show the world the reality of Castro's regime, the misery and exploitation of the Cuban people.

The following essay: "Bolivia: The Plurinational State´s Constitution is Void and Null" a very well-written, well-informed essay and iconic analysis on the need to enable, attract and promote convert to act without fear against a "de-facto" government. Despite of loosing the February 21st, 2016 referendum, the government is jostling to secure the President's indefinite tenure in power. The current Constitution is part of the so-called "October Agenda". It allows President Morales to suppress democratic institutions, to take control over the Judicial Branch, and to cover up the economic crisis, corruption and drug dealing. According to Sanchez Berzain, this Constitution is null, void, the Government acts are criminal, and the Bolivian people know it. The precise contribution of this essay is to open a path to the range and level of discourse beyond the immediate context.

The next two essays "Of Stubborn History and Tectonic Fault lines: learning from history to rebuild

Venezuela" and "Why Democracy is Not a Choice but a Necessity" focus on the situation of Democracy in the region, especially in Venezuela.

The first one is about understanding the progress and collapses of the Caribbean country. Rangel, frames the issue of devising a plan that addresses the fault lines and fosters the development of a more resilient institutional framework that can grow with the country's social and economic development. Finally, it concludes on the importance of the vision of national sovereignty as a strong legal state that is built on democracy. Moreover, legal states mean a more stable and safer region. Therefore Democracy is not a choice, but a necessity, and it is the obligation of OAS members to fight for it and strengthen it.

The second one has precious data and statistics on the situation of democracy in Ecuador and Venezuela. Fleischman further develops the concepts of democracy, sovereignty and legality, which are essential elements for a more stable region. He concludes that National sovereignty cannot become the principle that protects a usurper of societal power or his right to destroy a much-needed legality.

Finally, Cesar Vidal's essay: "Pandora's Box - 2017", makes a remarkable analysis and a prediction of what the 2017 will attain. On his personal point of view this year will be very dynamic and fraught with uncertainty. The geopolitical picture is turning really worrying and not at all encouraging, according to Vidal.

These essays are originated and focus on concrete circumstances that we are facing today. This gives them a distinctive quality, and renders the opinions a status of manuscript for a political understanding. I invite all to read these, and critically draw your own conclusions.

The knowledge of these causes and dissemination of publications presented by these experts provides an effective contribution to the defense of democratic values.

THE ANATOMY OF RACISM

For Mario Kreutzberger, Don Francisco,
who wondered where racism came from.

By Carlos Alberto Montaner[*]

Rep. Steve King, an Iowa Republican, tweeted: We can't restore our civilization with somebody else's babies." A contrary view came from two Cuban-American representatives, also Republican, Carlos Curbelo and Ileana Ros-Lehtinen. Ileana was specific: "Diversity is our strength." The clash was reported by *El Nuevo Herald.*

Therein lies the core of a permanent debate: human, i.e., animal nature, espoused by King, opposed to the artificial rationality that has emerged in the course of our civilization. Uniformity against diversity. Genetic links *versus* relations founded on the law. The logic of race, of blood, of Hitler, against the logic of natural rights and, if you wish, the logic of the Judeo-Stoic-Christian tradition.

True, racism is on the rise worldwide. This is demonstrated in the growing episodes of anti-Semitism. It's happening in France, Holland, Spain, Italy. The slogan "Make America Great Again" is not only an economic or indus-

---

[*] Journalist and writer.

trial issue, it's making the U. S. once again essentially white, northern European and uniformly English-speaking, the way Representative King would like it to be.

That's how the American ruling class was when the republic was founded in the late 18th Century, a mythical golden age when the Founding Fathers came together. That's how it was until an African-American gentleman named Barack Hussein Obama came to the White House as the nation's 44th president.

That narrow definition of the United States may today include (though to a lesser degree) Jewish-Americans, Italian-Americans, Greek-Americans and the rest of the expatriates who have immigrated *en masse* to the United States in the past 150 years, but the hard nucleus of U. S. identity, the ethnic group that generates the strongest stereotype is the mythical Anglo-Saxon enthused by Donald Trump's victory as, for example, Congressman Steve King, the descendant of the Irish, the Germans and the Welsh.

Racism is a feature inherent to human nature. Children are born without experiencing it, and evolve that way during the first years of their lives, until they gradually acquire an identity. That's the point of no return. As soon as the *id* defines itself and takes root, it triggers a blind impulse to segregate or liquidate the others, the different ones, those who really are not part of its group or share its primary identity.

Identity makes us racists because we gradually cease to be individuals in the abstract and become part of a tribe that identifies itself by the color of the skin, the type of hair, the shape of the eyes, the language we use, the intonation of our speech, the gestures we use, the religious beliefs, the mythology or shared stories and a thousand other details that form and conform the members of each group.

Anthropologist José Antonio Jáuregui, an especially intelligent scholar, suspected that that behavior of "identitarian" closeness was part of a natural strategy that would enable the species to prevail in the complex and aggressive course of evolution.

People who are part of a tribe have better chances to reproduce and pass their genes on to their descendants. To do this, the brain guides us in the right direction by means of neurotransmitters that carry pleasure or pain stimuli. As Jáuregui put it, we are "slaves of our brains."

Nationalism and sports fanaticism —almost always twinned— are an expression of this phenomenon. (Some days ago, when the Catalonians won an improbable soccer game with five successive goals, seismographs in Barcelona recorded the triumph with one point on the Richter scale produced by the joyful leaps of tens of thousands of frenzied Barcelonians, suddenly united by the paroxysm provoked by the victory of the local team).

How could a *mestizo* with an Arab name and partially African origin win the presidency if societies remain bound by those ancient and invisible ties? Because, at least temporarily, the republican (in the good sense of the word) concept of the species had triumphed —we are all equal under the law. It was the triumph of republicanism, a blessed device based on the beautiful superstition that what makes Americans "American" is respect for the Constitution.

That's where we stand. Struggling against a million-years past, so that people won't be prejudged by the color of their skin, the gods to whom they pray, the sexual desires that dominate them and the rest of the elements that constitute their identity.

Eventually, all that will be achieved and we will expunge racism forever. But it will take a long time for reason to win that combat. After all, we were animals for millions of years and it was only 25 centuries ago in Athens that Zeno the Stoic, a red-haired foreigner, small and knock-kneed, dared to say that people had rights beyond parentage and place of birth. A mere while ago.

HUMAN RIGHTS IN CUBA

By Armando Valladares[*]

Cuba is the largest island of the Antilles, discovered by Christopher Columbus in 1492. It is 90 miles from the Florida peninsula in the U.S.A., and currently has about 11 million inhabitants. One-sixth of the population lives abroad where they have been fleeing from the repression of the Cuban government. There are two irrefutable facts that I want to mention before developing the subject of human rights in the island: the first is that Cuba has had a dictatorship for over fifty years. It is the longest dictatorship that an American country has suffered, and perhaps the longest compared to any other dictatorship throughout the planet… There is no good dictatorship no matter what sign or ideology it is. From the ethical point of view, all dictatorships are condemnable and there should be no difference between a torture session in a dictatorship on the right or in a dictatorship on the left (communist). However, in the case of Cuba, a selective sensitivity has prevailed, a double standard that has translated into complicit support for the lack of all freedoms, the systematic violation of human rights, torture, dispossession and the

____

* Poet, painter, diplomat, and human rights activist.

most brutal repression that Cuba has ever known. The reason for this support that Castro has received, which has allowed him to repress with absolute impunity, to bury his victims in silence, to kill, has succeeded thanks to his confrontation and aggression against the United States. The vast majority of countries and their governments, intellectuals, individuals, and the press, hate the U.S. This hatred has been channeled through Castro's crimes in the moral aberration of believing that with that support of the communist dictator and his methods against "Yankee imperialism", hits Americans in the head. And the second fact, also irrefutable, is that the tyrant Fidel Castro has always lied. Note that in 1959, in the famous program 'Ante la Prensa' in the United States, he declared that he was not a communist and that he was against communism and any dictatorship.

On April 2nd, 1959, in statements to Cuban television Castro said: "to persecute the Catholic because he is a Catholic, to persecute the Protestant because he is Protestant, to persecute the Mason because he is a Mason, to persecute the Rotary because he is a Rotarian, to chase the Journal of Marina because it is a right-wing newspaper, or to persecute another because it is of left-wing, one because it is radical and of extreme right and another of extreme left, I do not conceive, nor will the revolution… democratic is what we are doing, respect all ideas. When you start by closing a newspaper, no newspaper can feel safe; when you start chasing a man for his political ideas, no one can feel safe."

Not even the most fervent accomplices of the Castro dictatorship can deny these statements. Castro lied because for a Marxist, the end justifies the means. And thousands of Cubans were and are persecuted for their ideas, shot and imprisoned, newspapers were closed, and a communist dictatorship established. Everything he said he would never do the revolution.

In 1959 the vast majority of the Cuban people supported Fidel Castro. His struggle against the dictatorship of Fulgencio Batista had much support and sympathy. It was the time when Castro promised justice, freedom and respect for the dignity of the human being. That deception lasted for a short time because Castro did nothing other than replace the dictatorship which he fought, by his own dictatorship, a thousand times more bloodthirsty with more than 15 thousand shot and tenths of thousands killed in political and military prisons or tortured in the Headquarters of the political and military jails, the terrible headquarters of State Security in whose basements, thousands of Cubans have lost their lives.

When many of those who supported him and fought in the mountains in the famous guerrilla war, the entrepreneurs and capitalists who financed the revolution but who had not done so to establish a communist dictatorship began to disagree with Castro, they ended up leaving their lives in the walls of execution, in prison or fleeing the country.

Among the best known and closest to Castro were Commander Huber Matos, who fought alongside him in the Sierra Maestra and only by refusing to continue in the Revolution; without being involved in any conspiracy or counterrevolutionary activity, for the mere fact of writing a letter to Castro saying that he did not want to continue in the government, he was accused of traitor and condemned to 20 years of prison, which he fulfilled until the last day. The same happened to the commander Mario Chanes; he was one of the assailants to the Moncada Barracks, served prison with Castro, trained in Mexico and returned to Cuba on the yacht Granma, the armed expedition that started the war in the mountains of the Sierra Maestra. In the first years of the revolution by not supporting Castro and opposing his communist plans, Chanes was sentenced to 30 years in prison, which he also served until the last day.

Other ex-comrades of Castro ran with worse luck, because they were executed in front of the firing squares like commanders: Sori Marín, Jesus Carreras, Clodomiro Miranda, William Morgan and many others.

Human rights violations began in January 1959 between the 8th and 9th of that month, in the province of Oriente, on the hill of San Juan, 103 soldiers were killed, without trial, and without specific charges. Among them were ten young men who aspired to be soldiers and were there waiting to be examined for approval or not. Castro's rebels, led by his brother Raul and other officers of the triumphant revolution, opened a bulldozer trench and on the edge placed the victims who fell dead to the mass grave when the firing squads executed them.

Two witnesses remained, one of them Carlos Lazo Cuba, a former member of the Air Force who now lives in the city of Miami, whom they separated at the last minute to try him in a judicial process that prepared these soldiers. This one took place in 1959, and it was the famous trial to the pilots of the overthrow Air force of the government of Batista. A revolutionary tribunal composed of bearded combatants failed to find a single test against those men, simply because they were mechanics, ground personnel, liaison pilots, mailers, etc., since those who could be accused of attacking the guerrillas of Castro in the mountains — otherwise lawful in a war — had fled the country in their own airplanes.

When Fidel Castro learned that they had been acquitted, he became angry and demanded that they be retried and that everyone should be sentenced to 30 years in prison. The revolutionary commander, who served as a Public Prosecutor, a bearded man with a true sense of honor, was so ashamed of that juridical monstrosity that he preferred to shoot himself in the head rather than to re-prosecute those men for the same accusations. His name was Felix Eleuterio Pena.

Thus began the violations of Human Rights in Cuba in the month of January 1959. All the high officials who in that revolutionary government were silent in the face of these abuses and crimes were somehow accomplices active or passive. Prisoners were shot, accused of the death of a revolutionary who days later appeared to be alive because he was exiled in Venezuela or in another country. Crimes were committed, summary judgments without procedural guarantees, without evidence, and condemned by conviction. The then chief of the military fortress of the Cabaña, was the famous commander "Ché" Guevara, who said "if in doubt, you must shoot". Himself, with his own hands, with his own weapon, executed dozens of prisoners, and the most famous was Lieutenant Castaño, who was taken from the cell, seated in the front seat of a military jeep, behind was Ché Guevara who killed him by shooting him in the back of the neck.

When speaking in international organizations, reports of non-governmental organizations dealing with violations of human rights in Cuba, statistics are cited. Those academic reports, cold... in my opinion, are more than figures, they are my ghosts, they are my deceased, and they are the men with whom I shared more years than those I lived with my own blood sister. That is why my testimony of the human rights situation is not a journalistic story, nor an analysis from the outside, with codes and pieces and citations of the laws violated: I am a first-hand witness, a protagonist and a victim.

I was an official of the revolutionary government of Fidel Castro. I worked in the Ministry of Communications, and I was then a 21-year-old boy who also believed in that bearded, charismatic man. I believed in all that torrent of promises of peace, social justice, of liberty and happiness for all Cubans. My ideals as an adolescent made me see it as the solution to all the problems of the Nation ... But that illusion lasted very little ... I had ideological training and deep Christian beliefs ... and from within, I witnessed how the communists were occupying the key positions of power. Castro was still denying his Marxist militancy...

One morning militiamen from the government, armed with machine guns, showed up at my office to place a sign on my desk with a slogan that said: "If Fidel is a communist, put me on the list because I agree with him." That was the offensive propaganda of the Communist Party, based on the reasoning that if everything that Fidel made was good for the people, and if it was communism, then being a communist was not bad, and if Fidel was one, why wasn't I too? The ideologues of the Party thought that the population, the multitudes, would react like that, but I did not accept putting that slogan on my table. The militiaman asked me in a menacing tone why didn't I agree with Fidel… and "if he's a communist, then no" was my answer. I did not suspect the transcendence of my refusal, but it was sufficient to point me out as dissatisfaction, as an enemy of the revolution…

A few weeks later I woke up with the barrel of a machine gun on my forehead pushing my head against the pillow. It was the early morning of December 28th of 1960. In a meticulous search carried out in my house, they found nothing that could point me as a conspirator, no weapons, no explosives, no counterrevolutionary fliers, nothing…

They took me to the headquarters of the Political Police. During the interrogations the officers informed me that although they had no evidence against me, and although no one accused me, they had the moral conviction that I was a potential enemy of the Revolution and that they would condemn me. In one week I was in front of a Revolutionary Court in the military fortress of the Cabaña. The President of that People's Court had his legs crossed on the table, and in a gesture of contempt for what was happening, he was reading a comics magazine, I could only see the soles of his boots.

In fact, he did not have to pay attention, because the sentences were already issued from the headquarters of the State Security, there where they imposed the sentences. When a prisoner had a lawyer with good relationships within the government, before going to court, he could tell his client how many years he would receive in sentence. In just one week from the date of my arrest, I had been "investigated" "prosecuted", sentenced to 30 years of imprisonment, and 20 years of political interdiction.

When I returned to the prison yard, my prison mates lifted me on their shoulders and congratulated me. For an observer outside this reality, it may seem surreal to congratulate a prisoner who had just been sentenced to 30 years in prison. The reason for that congratulation was because —in those days— they were only giving two sentences: 30 years in prison or the death penalty, and I had saved my life…

In a few days I was transferred to the prison on Isla de Pinos, an island in the south of Cuba, which inspired Robert Louis Stevenson to write "The Treasure Island" In October of 1961, along with three other prison mates, we escaped from the prison. One of them was Pedro Luis Boitel, a university student leader and combat partner of Fidel Castro. Years later, while Pedro Luis was on a hunger strike, Fidel Castro himself gave the order to deny him water until he died. Pedro Luis died in terrible agony.

Three days later we were captured. I had a leg very swollen by the breakage of several bones. We were taken to punishment cells and when I asked for medical assistance for my blackened leg, a guard smashed it. The guards walked above the dungeons, which had steel mesh roofs, and punctured us with wooden and from above they pricked us with pointed wooden sticks to keep us from sleeping. One of the punishments consisted in throwing us, from above, containers filled with urine and excrement collected among common crimes prisoners. We would wake up with our faces covered in shit and dripping urine. There was no water, and we spent a year without being able to bathe. Fidel Castro declared back then: that the revolution had never mistreated a prisoner.

There, we were victims of all kinds of tortures, systematic beatings, incommunicado for years. I am a survivor of the forced labor plans of Isla de Pinos. When the crews went out into the fields at dawn, one never had the certainty of returning alive. Thousands were wounded, savagely beaten, tortured, killed in the quarries, in the swamplands. Those were real extermination camps.

Our complaints and those of our relatives to the international organizations were not heard. As the Cuban confrontation with the United States was increased; and the more support Cuba received from the press and from other governments, the more crueler they would be to us. Every time the Americans bombed the Communist guerrillas of Vietnam, the garrison of the prison was in full swing and they would beat us savagely.

From the prison of Isla de Pinos we were taken to the jail of Boniato. There, they had established a center for biologic experimentation ran by doctors from the communist Germany, Czechoslovakia and also Cubans. We were locked in cells with doors and windows completely covered with steel plates, with a slot at floor level where they opened a lid to slide the plates with the food, no running water, sleeping on the floor, in total solitary confinement, denying us medical care, correspondence, books, sunlight or artificial light, keeping us in constant darkness. For months we only received a diet based on only carbohydrates. They did so to cause deficiency diseases and metabolic disorders. The portions consisted of a mixture of corn flour, boiled pasta and rice. Our doctors there, also prisoners, estimated that it did not reach a thousand calories a day. Soon the results of that diet lacking of proteins and vitamins, began to be noticed. We were losing weight by the hour, by days. A few months later the first cases of scurvy appeared, a deficiency disease caused by the absence of vitamin C; some of them appeared as dark granites and bruises on the skin, arms and thighs. The gums swelled and reddened, and began to bleed by just touching them.

One of us, Engineer Arroyo, would press his gums with his thumb and blood would run all along his arm and dripping on the floor … his teeth loosened and he almost lost them all… The edema of hunger appeared. I remember that when my legs swelled, I would press a finger firmly on them and it would sink in as if it were on soft clay. Then there was an impressive gap from where the liquid of inflammation had moved.

The doctors would go to examine us from cell to cell, taking blood samples, interrogating us about how we felt, how we slept, what we thought, what we missed the most… they were experimenting with us. That lasted for weeks, for months, until Esteban Ramos Kessel appeared dead in his cell and a few days later Ibrahim Torres Martinez, both died of malnutrition. Later, due to lack of medical assistance, Ramón Castillo del Pozo died. Then the doctors distributed vitamin C and gave us some fruits and proteins… they did not want their guinea pigs to die… When the family of Esteban Ramos Kessel claimed his body, the communist authorities told them that this inmate had died without fulfilling his sentence, and that he owed years to the revolution, therefore his corpse belonged to them… It has never been known in which cemetery they buried this prisoner.

One day, maddened by a toothache, Laureano tried to extract the piece himself with a moldy nail and a spoon, but only managed to smash his gums and tear the tooth apart. Within a few hours he had an infection that Inflamed the entire jaw. The military was called but they refused to remove the prisoner and give him medical assistance. They promised to give him an injection for the pain, but they didn't. The next day they did not do it either. Prisoners in protest rejected the lunch. An officer and head of the building, Lieutenant Elio, came to say that they would only give him assistance if he accepted political rehabilitation, if he signed a document denying his ideals. The prisoners did all they could to save the life of Laureano, who by then had a high fever and began a septicemia: they started shaking the prison bars violently. The guards came, and the prisoners were taken from cell to cell, with kicks, breaking their heads with iron bars, until they were being pushed to the end of the corridor. Lieutenant Perez de la Rosa, chief of that fiery troop, was beating the prisoner Enrique Diaz Correa, and another prisoner, Preacher Gerardo Gonzalez, was interposed between them, whom we all affectionately called the Brother of the Faith. He raised his arms to the sky —as he always did— and said: "Forgive them Lord, they do not know what they do!" He asked God for forgiveness for his executioners… it was in a fraction of a second; Lieutenant Perez de la Rosa shot a blast with his machine gun, which almost separated his head from his body. The Brother of the Faith fell instantly dead, behind him Enrique Diaz Correa tried to hold the body, the lieutenant shot again and Enrique received nine shots from that second burst until the day of his death, because he was saved on that occasion. He carried a projectile lodged in his back.

When that massacre was reported to the non-governmental organization Amnesty International, the response our relatives received from them was that the Cuban government (the dictatorship) had given them a different version from the one we had given. It was the year of 1975. Thousands of Cuban political prisoners had already been killed on the firing squads, tried without due process guarantees, prosecuted without evidence, hundreds of extrajudicial executions had taken place, forced labor had ended on the Isle of Pines with the aftermath of thousands of Political prisoners beaten, tortured, murdered, maddened… the nightmare of the biological experiments of the Boniato jail was finished with those killed there and left behind… Castro had already ordered the death of Pedro Luis Boitel, they had already assassinated student Alfredo Carrión, Ernesto Díaz Madruga, Roberto López Chávez, who was denied water and when he was agonizing for it, almost unconscious on the floor, four soldiers came, and they asked him if he was thirsty and then they urinated him in the face and mouth. He died the next day…

None of this was what Amnesty International wanted to believe or investigate, for them in all those years, in Cuba there were no political prisoners, much less violations of human rights. Sean McBride was then Secretary General of Amnesty International. This man led over a conference on Human Rights in Caracas, Venezuela, to which they had invited my wife… When she began to speak and mentioned the Cuban political prisoners, Sean McBride began to pound the microphone so that no one could hear what she said. He shouted and demanded that they not let her talk... That same year, 1977, Sean McBride received the Lenin Peace Medal, granted by the Central Committee of the Communist Party of the then Soviet Union... Fidel Castro's Communist Cuba was non-existent for the prestigious organization that defended human rights. It was in 1978 that when Amnesty International, without Sean McBride's leadership, "discovered" that there were political prisoners in Cuba. I was the first prisoner of conscience adopted by this organization in which marvelous and kind people work for, but its leadership is generally formed by elements of the extreme left, that can not hide, although they try, their sympathy for the dictatorship of Fidel Castro.

The fervor and the immediate denunciation when it came to human rights violations in Pinochet's Chile or the Argentina of the military coup, would cool off when it came to denunciations of the Cuban dictatorship. The Cubans almost had to show the corpses. Amnesty would ask the dictatorship and they were inclined to believe Castro's denials.

The violation of Human Rights in Cuba is constitutional. I believe it is the only country that admits the violation of Human Rights in its Magna Carta. For example, Article 52 of the Cuban Constitution states that: "There is freedom of expression and of the press according to the aims of the socialist society..." The Inter-American Commission on Human Rights published an analysis of this article of the Cuban Constitution, which I reproduce here:

> As it can be seen, the Cuban Constitution subordinates
> the exercise of freedom of expression "for the purpo-

ses of the socialist society." It is not a question of the limitations usually stipulated in other constitutions, such as public order, morality and good manners, the rights of others or the safeguarding of the reputation of people, etc. Limitations to the exercise of human rights are always essential, what is different —and decisive— is the perspective from which these limitations are established.

In one case, they obey the need to harmonize the exercise of different rights and ensure, in this way, the validity of all of them: The role of the State is to achieve this harmonization in concrete situations restricting the exercise of rights only with that end. In the case of the Constitution of Cuba that is considered, the perspective is different: it is the exercise of rights that must be adapted to the goals that the State seeks to achieve. In one case, it is the State that limits its action against the rights of the people; In the case under examination, it is the individuals who limit their rights to the purposes pursued by the State.

Artistic freedom is also limited by the Constitution, in article 38, which says: "artistic creation is permitted, provided that its content is not contrary to the Revolution." This is the legal justification for censorship. But who determines that the artistic work is contrary to the Revolution? What does it mean, contrary to the Revolution? This constitutional violation of artistic freedom was further demonstrated by the famous words of the dictator Fidel Castro to the intellectuals when he said: "within the Revolution, everything, outside the Revolution, nothing." The

UNEAC (National Union of Writers and Artists of Cuba) has been the censoring apparatus, the police of the artists. I remember the case of a University professor suspected of being dissatisfied with the Revolution, who had his house searched and they grabbed a book, "The Prophecies of Nostradamus" written in 1500, because although it seems unbelievable, they gave the book to the "Intellectuals of the UNEAC," and these, after deep studies and analysis, ruled that the book was "anti-Cuban and anti-Soviet". The university professor was sentenced to 6 years in prison for the possession of that "counterrevolutionary" book.

In 1988, at the 56th Assembly of Human Rights of the United Nations, it was agreed that a commission should travel to Cuba to investigate the situation of Human Rights on the Island.

Ambassador Alione Sene of Senegal led the delegation. Ambassadors J.Sefi Attah of Nigeria, representing the group of African countries, Todor Dichev of the then communist Bulgaria, representing the countries behind the iron curtain, the Deputy Secretary for Foreign Affairs Jose D. English of the Philippines, representing the Asian countries, Michael J. Lillis of Ireland, representing the western bloc countries, Rafael Rivas Posada de Colombia, representing the countries of Latin America.

At last, the dream of many Cubans who were victims of torture and violations of human rights in Cuba to bring the issue to the United Nations had been achieved. Now it was only necessary that Cuba could not manipulate the result of the investigation. The Cuban Ambassador, Raul Roa had assured Fidel Castro that he had everything under control. I, myself, listened to his telephone conversations with the dictator. The Cuban government underestimated the ambassadors that made up the commission and forgot that opponents of the dictatorship could also think and act.

The eleven-day work on the island was compiled in a report of four hundred pages. It was the first time that a country was so thoroughly investigated in all aspects of society. It was the most comprehensive report ever made by the United Nations in its history and the irrefutable proof that Cuba violates Human Rights in a systematic and institutional way.

The group managed to document in those eleven days, 137 (one hundred and thirty-seven) cases of torture, seven people missing, 128 arbitrary arrests, 102 violations of the right to due process, 199 to the right to security, 81 violations of religious freedom, 45 to freedom of association, 146 violations of economic, social and cultural rights, 264 violations of the right to work and its enjoyment, Political assassinations and thousands of violations of all the articles of the Universal Declaration of Human Rights, of which Cuba is a signatory. (Pages 103, 104 and 105 of Report E / CN.4 / 1989/46, February 21, 1989)

The report of that commission also quotes in paragraph 75 (seventy-five) some types of torture: Hereinafter, I transcribe that paragraph:

Confinement in cold rooms, lack of control in time and space, immersion in blind wells, bullying with dogs, simulation of executions, beating prisoners, forced labor, confinement for years in dungeons called "drawers", the use of loudspeakers with deafening noises during hunger strikes, depersonalization of the detainee through total nudity in punishment cells, water suppression for prisoners declared on hunger strikes, presentation of the naked inmate to their relatives to force them to accept the political rehabilitation plan, denial of medical care for an indefinite period of time and obligation imposed on the person sentenced to death to load his own coffin and dig his own grave before being shot.

This UN report, supported by irrefutable evidence, showed that torture in Cuba exists, that there are missing persons and that human rights are being violated. The discussion of this report lasted several days. The Ambassador of England, Henry Steel, declared in the Assembly that this report was the irrefutable proof that in Cuba the 30 articles of the Universal Declaration of Human Rights were violated, and that the whole social and political structure of Cuban society was in contradiction with each and every one of said articles. Cuba lost the subsequent vote and was seated on the bench of the defendants where it should have been since 1959.

This report of the UN Commission on Human Rights is available to those who want to see it or have it; they only have to ask the Commission.

In order to update this analysis of the human rights situation in Cuba, I want to include the last Amnesty International report of 2008:

Freedom of expression, association and circulation continued to be severely restricted. At least 62 prisoners of conscience remained in prison and political dissidents, independent journalists and human rights activists continued to suffer harassment, intimidation and imprisonment...

On freedom of expression and association, Amnesty International denounces that:

All media, printed and audiovisual, remained under state control. During 2007, the government decided not to renew the visas of several foreign correspondents because its "way of approaching the Cuban situation is not the one that best suits the Cuban government."

Here we must remember article 52 of the Cuban Constitution that says: "There is freedom of expression and of the press according to the aims of socialist society." As these journalists do not write according to the ends of the government, they simply expel them from the country. All those who remain in Cuba are because they "please" the dictatorship and they put their pens at the service of tyranny.

In Cuba there are two surrealist laws that have no comparison with anything even resembling. They are the laws of predictive danger and of post-criminal danger. I will explain what this legal monstrosity means in the life of the Cubans of the Island: According to this law, any authority, police, and member of the Ministry of Interior etc., interprets that any citizen, by the time he comes to his house, by the way he dresses, by the friendships he has etc., is about to commit a crime, (not committed). It is an appreciation of the Police who becomes kind of a fortuneteller of the revolution, and to avoid that that citizen commits the crime, they imprison him for at least one year under the protection of this law of predictive danger. There is no trial, there is no legal process of any kind, the police do not have to give any explanation to any superior, they simply fill out a form, they elevate it to the competent authorities, and then they go to the citizen's house and take him to prison. It's that simple. This law has served to satisfy personal revenge, to remove from the way a husband who can be an obstacle to the police who wants the wife of this one, and especially to lock down critics of the government. The application of the law of post-criminal danger is applied to inmates who serve their sentences and the authorities read that he is not fit to join the new socialist society, and is left there for a year or two more. Many of my colleagues, those who did not accepted the political rehabilitation when they fulfilled their original sentences, served the double of years due to that law.

Let's look at what Amnesty International says about this dangerous law in its 2008 report:

Social Hazard. The criminal justice system continued to be used to silence political dissidents and critics of the government. Numerous people were convicted of the crime of "social danger". Figure <predictive> defined as the <proclivity in which a person is found to commit crimes>. This legislation penalizes, for example, drunkenness, addiction to drugs and antisocial behavior. However, it was applied almost exclusively to political dissidents, independent journalists and critics with the government. Persons convicted of <social

dangerousness> were facing up to four years in prison and could be subjected to <therapeutic>, <reeducate> and <surveillance by the National Revolutionary Police (PNR).

Arbitrary detentions have been practiced by the Cuban dictatorship since 1959, and there is still a constant violation of human rights, as Amnesty International says in its 2008 report:

> **Arbitrary detentions.** Political dissidents, independent journalists and government detractors continued to be harassed for carrying out dissident activities or reporting on the human rights situation in Cuba. Some were released after being detained for 24-48 hours, while others were held in prison for months or even years awaiting trial.

On the death penalty, Amnesty International reported that:

> About forty people were still condemned to death. The last execution known to Amnesty International took place in April 2003...

Religious freedom in Cuba

In the report of the working group that visited Cuba, in page number 293, Annex XXV is the copy of the indictment to the Cuban citizen Ruben Hoy Ruiz, whose trial was held in Sagua La Grande. The Court was composed of Luisa Y. Vázquez Guerra, President of the court and judges Raúl Pérez Herrera and Pedro H. Izquierdo. The trial was number 325 of 1981, concerning offenses and possession of unauthorized printed material.

The serious crime of this Cuban citizen was that they occupied a Bible and a book of the New Testament. Those were the unauthorized printed materials. He was sentenced to nine months of imprisonment and nine more months with the loss of all his citizens' rights, including, of course, the rationing card. To convict him, the court referred to Article 374, paragraph 9, sub-paragraph (2). The date of the sentence was: May 16th, 1985, which was signed by the secretary of the courts Abelardo Reyes Perez.

The Christian Solidarity Worldwide Organization (CSW) reports on religious freedom in Cuba and says in its annual report that:

> During the past year dramatic reports of violations of religious freedom in Cuba have increased dramatically. It is for this increase that the CWA calls for the re-examination of this problem by the United Nations' Human Rights Council as part of its periodic review in the near future. We believe that this request is particularly relevant in light of the fact that Cuba has signed the International Covenant on Civil and Political Rights (ICCPR) and the International Covenant on Economic, Social and Cultural Rights (ICESRC) in March of 2008. While this Act was a significant movement on the part of the Cuban government, the provisions of the two conventions regrettably have not been reflected in the legislation or in the behavior of the authorities.

Instead, violations of freedom of religion grew substantially, in addition to other rights allegedly guaranteed under those conventions and the Universal Declaration of Human Rights.

(A note of the author of this piece). (A few days after the Cuban government signed these protocols, in the middle of the street, in the presence of international journalists, they brutally beat a group of dissidents including Dr. Darsi Ferrer.)

The CWS report continues:

Violations of religious freedom over the past year vary in severity from threats and the intimidating presence of state security agents in religious gatherings to the confiscation of church buildings and / or Houses, eviction of pastors and their families and in a couple of cases, physical destruction of the Churches. (Clarifying note of the author) These allegations do not include or affect the Catholic Church in Cuba which has been the church of complicit silence and collaboration with the dictatorship, to such point that when the UN commission visited Cuba, Bishop Jaime Ortega y Alamino said at least that human rights were violated in Cuba, but in an attitude of supreme cowardice, he flatly refused and that was the most that was accomplished (there were private efforts to explain the importance of that single phrase) was to declare that "in Cuba there were concessions, not rights."

The CWS report on the lack of religious freedom in Cuba continues:

Victims of these violations have included unregistered "house churches" and registered churches of members of the Council of Churches of Cuba (CIC) as well as outside the CIC group that traditionally enjoys preferential treatment from the government. In addition, since most of these violations took place in rural areas or in remote urban areas where communication with the rest of the Island or the world outside the Island becomes extremely difficult, it could indicate a much broader problem.

Another area of concern is the dissemination of government informants in churches, prayer and study groups and seminars. There were numerous reports by Pastors and other Church leaders of severe harassment, including death threats and incarceration, against religious leaders who publicly called for greater religious freedom and against those who refused to work on behalf of the authorities with informants Or to provide public support for government initiatives. In one case, the children of a pastor in a state of serious health did not receive medical treatment after the eviction of their houses and churches by Communist Party officials. Religious leaders of all denominations have complained of having faced difficulties with applications for exit visas or permits for Church vehicles.

As we have already seen in the case of a citizen convicted of possessing a Bible, which the authorities consider

"PRINTED MATERIAL NOT AUTHORIZED" the report of the organization Christian Solidarity denounces that:

> Another issue has been the hard restrictions of importing the Bible and other religious materials from the Cuban government. This restriction caused a severe shortage of these books and materials. These limitations stipulate, for example, that the importation of all types of religious literature, including the Bible, has to go through CIC's internal control, despite the fact that CIC represents only a minority of Protestant Christians. Catholics have also commented on the lack of the Bible and the difficulties involved in importing religious materials. The continued use of these restrictions on the importation of religious material by the government goes against the idea of the two United Nations conventions signed earlier this year.

With regard to religious repression against political prisoners, this report states that:

> In a separate case, however related to the subject, relatives of political prisoners continue to report that prison officials arbitrarily deny political prisoners their right to practice basic religious freedoms protected by the Standard Rules of Minimal Treatment of United Nations prisoners. Prisoners also reported that Bibles and other religious materials had been confiscated, and sometimes, returned to only be confiscated again on the grounds of increasing pressure on prisoners.

One of the worst crimes was committed against families trying to escape from Cuba in a Tug Boat. This fact, well known around the world, thanks to the departure of the country of some of the survivors, is known as the case of the *Tug 13 of March.*

We transcribed Report No. 47/96 of the Inter-American Commission of Human Rights of the Organization of American States.

"Victims of the Tug Boat 'March 13' vs. Cuba", Case 11.436. Report No.47/96. Imter-Am., OEA / Ser.L / VII.95 Doc. 7 rev.en 127 (1997).

Victims of the tug boat "13 of march" vs Cuba

Background

1. On July 19th, 1994, the Inter-American Commission on Human Rights received a complaint that, in the hours of dawn of July 3rd of 1994, four ships belonging to the Cuban state and equipped with water hoses struck an old tugboat that fled Cuba with 72 people on board. The incident occurred seven miles away from the Cuban coast, in front of the port of the city of Havana. The abovementioned complaint also states that the vessels of the Cuban state attacked their respective bows to the fugitive tugboat with the intention of sinking it. At the same time, all the people on the ship's deck, including women and children, were being water pressured. The plea of the women and children to stop the attack was in vain, as the old boat, called "March 13" sank with a death toll of 41, of which 10 were minors, 31 people survived the events of 13 July 1994.

2. On February 28th of 1995, the Inter-American Commission on Human Rights received another complaint on the same facts, which was filed to case No.11.436, in accordance with article 53 of its rules of procedure.

The report of this Commission is very extensive, so I will only transcribe some of its paragraphs, which will serve to have a general idea of this violation of life committed by the Cuban government.

> 51. An interesting fact is that the survivors identify the aggressive tugs as the MININT (Ministry of the Interior). This Ministry has as its functions, the affairs of the police, state security and law enforcement agencies of the Cuban State. This shows that, the repressive forces of the dictatorship committed the crime. Moreover, centralism is one of the characteristics of the system. No great decision can be taken without the approval of Castro or a high state body. This case is no exception, given the fact of the presence of the stalking element and the type of organism involved. In this act there had to be planning and direction by higher state bodies.

> 52. There are elements of conduct that evidence this argument. It is customary for the Cuban State, when acts of repudiation and aggression against the opponents (see the case of the poet Maria Elena Cruz Varela) to use agents of the Department of State Security dressed in civilian clothes, together with cadres of the Communist Party and Union of Young Communists. This attack against defenseless civilians was planned, orchestrated and directed by the Communist Party and State Security and had the direct participation of both elements.

53. At the hearing before the Inter-American Commission on Human Rights dated September 7th of 1995, the petitioners stated inter alia that: "We have no doubt that at dawn of July 13th of 1994, the 72 persons who left the Havana Bay, seizing the old wooden tugboat and fleeing Cuba in search of the freedom denied there, were pursued and their boat struck by three more modern tugs of the Cuban Government; and this happened as soon as they left the bay. At the same time as they were doing these maneuvers they also threw powerful jets of water against the people who were on the deck of the tug '13 of March', who pleaded that there were children on board and to not continue to throw water on them or hit the boat, that they surrendered and would returned to Cuba. At the end, at 7 miles away from the Cuban coast, a stern thrust caused the '13 of March' tug to sink."

54. In order to complete the spectacle, the tugboats of the Cuban government revolved around the people who floated to make them swoop to sink and continued to throw jets of water under pressure. The balance of this abominable crime of this genocide was 41 dead, including several children. Three days after the events, some of the 31 survivors were rescued by other vessels of the Cuban Government, and not by tugs. The first thing the Cuban government did was to take these survivors as prisoners and two days later they released the women and children. It is noteworthy the testimony provided in Havana by survivor María Victoria García Suárez once she was on the street. The interview was managed to get out of Cuba WSCV by channel 51. The

television images of this woman crying and accusing the Cuban government shocked the public. María Victoria García Suárez, still in Cuba, narrated how she lost her husband, her 10-year-old son, her brother, three uncles, and two cousins.

55. Later, other eyewitnesses such as Janet Hernández, from inside of Cuba, lost their fear of government repression and reported the truth of the events abroad. It is important to point out to this illustrious Commission that the testimonies given in different dates and places coincide, which proves the absolute veracity of the crime committed by the Cuban government.

56. The first reaction of the government of Cuba through its representative in the Section of Interests in Washington, D.C. Mr. Rafael Dausá, was to qualify as 'science fiction' the testimonies of the survivors. On July 15th of 1994, the government of Cuba, through Mr. Dausá, said that the tugboat "13 of March" "had not sailed in 9 years due to its terrible conditions. "I could not do a miracle", Dausá said, "It sank because of its poor technical conditions. The irresponsible attitude of these pirates caused the incident." (See article on the newspaper El Nuevo Herald of Florida of Saturday July 16th of 1994).

84. The evidence clearly demonstrates that the sinking of the tugboat '13 of March' was not an accident, but a premeditated and intentional act. In fact, Jorge Hernández, survivor of the events that occurred on July 13th of 1994, states that: "When leaving el Morro, boats N.1, 2 assault them" and "offshore they began to be attacked by boats N.1 2, 3 And 5". That, "the tugboat

they were on received blows to port and starboard" and that, "they attacked them with jets of water". "After the last onslaught, the boat sinks because they had destroyed the stern." Finally, "tugboats did not help them", but "they told them to swim to the coast guard." Meanwhile, Archimedes Lebrigio states that: "when the boat sailed, he was in the lower part of the boat and could see that they were hit by the bow and stern." María Victoria García Suárez points out that: "in that we see that two firefighter tugboats are coming behind us, they stick to the sides and then they start throwing water at us." "Then we went on and we told them not to hurt us, we had children there and we showed them the children, but they kept throwing water. Then we saw two more [ships] and they put one on each side and then, the four of them began to throw water at us, and one of the ships crashed with us…" Finally, the witness states that: "there were the four tugboats —the ones that were sinking us— and we told them to save us, to get us up, that we had children, and they only laughed.

83. Finally, Jeanette Hernández Gutiérrez states that, "as we were leaving the bay, we see two tugboats being turned off at the mouth of the bay. They let us out, but then the jets from the water hoses started, they were constant, they didn't stop the jets even knowing that there were kids." "When we were seven miles away, we saw them accelerate to stand on our sides and started staggering us, we raised the children, they see them, and we started yelling at them to please stop what they were doing, but they didn't." "They, at any moment, told us with the loudspeaker to stop or

anything." Jeanette goes on to point out that, "we get a tugboat from behind, the biggest one… it goes over our stern and then breaks our boat in half." "When this happen the boat is drifting because the captain, named Fidencio Ramel, got knocked overboard from the pressure of the jets of water." "They sank when: the tug that leaves the stern is put forward and goes up in the bow and it breaks it." And finally she said that, "these tugboats back off, disappear from there for a few meters, but they do not throw us lifeguards —nothing—, they do not give us any type of help."

84. The Inter-American Commission on Human Rights must point out that, although it is true that the intentionality and premeditation of the material authors of the sinking of the tugboat "13 of March" has been fully demonstrated, it is also true that such intentionality is irrelevant in determining the international responsibility of the Cuban State. What is fundamental in the present case is to determine if the violation of the right to life has taken place with the support or tolerance of the State or if it has acted in a way that the transgression has been fulfilled in the absence of any prevention or impunity.

Conclusions

105. The State of Cuba is responsible for violating the right to life — Article I of the American Declaration of the Rights and Duties of the Man— of the 41 persons who were shipwrecked and died as a result of the sinking of the tugboat "13 of March", events occurred seven miles away from the Cuban coasts on July 13th of 1994.

Today, when I am finishing this project, it is December 11th, 2008. The news of the repression in Cuba, trying to prevent the dissidents on the island to celebrate International Human Rights Day and the 6th anniversary of the signing of that Declaration, fill newspapers around the world. I will cite some of the incidents reported by the press and non-governmental organizations that have reported these abuses:

Brutal beats to activists in Havana on the eve of the 60th anniversary of the Universal Declaration of Human Rights.

It happened at 1:05 p.m. on December 9th, on K Street between Linea and 13, in the neighborhood of Vedado, when 8 policemen in two patrol cars, commanded by a State Security officer (Political Police), brutally assaulted Belinda Salas Tápanes, Marlene Bermúdez, Lázaro Joaquín Alonso Román and Roberto Marrero. Without any conversation, the agents began to beat the activists with unprecedented violence, powerfully forcing them into patrol cars.

"They did not even ask for identification," said Belinda Salas, President of the Latin American Federation of Rural Women (FLAMUR). "My husband Lázaro received such a brutal beating that he bled abundantly through the mouth and head, and he received heavy blows to the testicles. Marlenis and her husband Roberto were beaten and the agents, while beating them, shouted that they would go directly to the province of Camagüey, where they reside. They broke my blouse leaving me naked, the blows fractured my hand, and they threw me out of the moving car."

Other organizations such as Human Rights Watch also denounced the repression of the Cuban government, saying in their statement:

According to HRW, security forces detained more than 30 people in the days leading up to International Human Rights Day. He added that many people were arrested while trying to travel to Havana to participate in marches and other activities scheduled for December 10th for the 60th anniversary of the Universal Declaration of Human Rights of the United Nations.

Human Rigths Watch indicated that, "according to their information, other dissidents were visited by security agents who warned them that they would be victims of beatings, imprisonment and other punishments if they participated in the commemoration activities."

Human Rights Watch demands from the Cuban government the "immediate and unconditional release of the detained dissidents.

This has become a pattern: the Cuban Government commemorates the Universal Declaration of Human Rights, violating its fundamental principles," denounced José Manuel Vivanco, Executive Director of the Americas division of Human Rights Watch.

Another non-governmental organization, Human Rights Foundation, issued a press note denouncing the repression on the eve of Human Rights Day.

The note says:

Cuba: The Castro government assaults, attacks and arrests human rights defenders. NEW YORK (December 11th, 2008). At least 20 activists have been threatened, beaten and detained this week in Cuba for planning celebrations for the 60th anniversary of the Universal Declaration of Human Rights (DUDH), as informed by Cuban sources. Among the detainees are: known dissidents, former political prisoners, human rights defenders and independent journalists. "The Raúl Castro government is threatening and arresting activists for the mere fact of wanting to applaud a human rights statement," said Sara Wasserman of the Human Rights Foundation (HRF). "It is clear that the pompous announcement by the Cuban government of the signing of the International Covenant on Civil and Political Rights at the beginning of this year is the highest hypocrisy, since despite the fact that the Cuban government continues to deny that in that country human rights violations are committed, the facts show the opposite...

I want to finish this analysis of the situation of human rights in Cuba with one of the two irrefutable facts that I pointed out at the beginning of this work: Fidel Castro lies.

"From our point of view, we have no human rights problems: there are no missing people here, there are no tortured people here, there are no murders here" (Fidel

Castro's statements to French and American journalists in the Palace of the Revolution in Havana on July 28th, 1983, as published in the newspaper Granma in the August 10th issue of the same year).

(Translated by Lizandra Garriga)

BOLIVIA: THE PLURINATIONAL STATE`S CONSTITUTION IS VOID AND NULL

The situation that makes Bolivia a victim today goes back to the so-called "October`s agenda", the political accord of October of 2003 to justify the overthrow of Bolivia`s constitutionally elected President Gonzalo Sanchez de Lozada through the so-called "gas war".

By Carlos Sanchez Berzaín[*]

In Bolivia, the jostling to secure the President`s indefinite tenure in power is underway –in spite of a resounding mandate in a referendum election of 21 February 2016 in which the people said NO. This is another Castroist-Chavist operation that seeks to continue simulating a democracy where none exists, placing at forefront a constitutional appeal so that its subjugated judges can manipulate the prohibition of reelection established by their constitution, which as a matter of fact, they have already violated twice before. There isn`t any possible legal way to enable Evo Morales to run again, or to legalize his government, because the entire constitutional

---

[*] Lawyer, writer, several times minister in Bolivia.

structure that enabled the existence of his regime is illegal, since the Constitution of his Plurinational State is devoid of lawful merit and is only a fragile façade of a "de-facto" government.

The situation that makes Bolivia a victim today goes back to the so-called "October`s agenda", the political accord of October of 2003 to justify the overthrow of Bolivia`s constitutionally elected President Gonzalo Sanchez de Lozada through the so-called "gas war". The new holders of power; Evo Morales, Carlos Mesa, Felipe Quispe, and others along with the so-called social movements, established as an objective of the triumphant conspirator move "the convening of a constituent assembly", "the nationalization of the oil based resources", "the persecution of the ousted government", "the disbandment of political parties", "anti-imperialism", and so on.

The Constitution of the Republic of Bolivia (CPE in Spanish) amended in 1994 –legal framework that was invoked to sign and implement the "October`s agenda" DOES NOT allow neither the "total amendment of the Constitution", nor the convening of a Constituent Assembly, because it institutes a system of "partial amendment" which starts with a law for the need to amend within the constitutional period of session that may be approved or rejected in the next constitutional period of session, this procedure was implemented to keep the reformers from benefitting from the amendments, especially when it came to the reelection of the President.

Bolivia`s constitution (CPE) ordains in its Article 230; "This constitution may be partially amended, with a prior declaration of the need to amend, which will be precisely mandated in legislation approved by two-thirds of the members present in each of the two houses" and in its Article 231 states; "The matter will be taken up in the first sessions of a new congressional session at the house that sponsored the legislation, and if it were to be approved by two-thirds of votes, it shall pass for review to the other house in which two-thirds of votes shall be required for approval". Complying with the aforementioned mandate, in August of 2002 (before the overthrow in October of 2003) legislation "for the need to amend the Constitution" would have been promulgated proposing the amendment of Articles 231, 232, and 233 within the "System of partial amendments of the Constitution" introducing the "Constitutional Referendum to approve or reject the amendment", in such a way that instead of approving the constitutional amendment only in Congress it would be done through a referendum.

To implement the "October`s agenda" the law for the need to amend of August of 2002 was used supplanting its content and leading to the promulgation of Law 2631 on 20 February of 2004 "To amend the Constitution" ignoring the requirement of legislation for the need to amend and introducing the "constituent assembly" for the "total change of the Constitution". Doing this they were committing falsehood, supplanting and violating the existing Constitution because a law to amend the constitution may only be "accepted or rejected" it is not modifiable and above it all "totally changing or amending the Constitution" is not allowed, and it is not possible. Therefore, Law 2631 of 2004 to amend the constitution is devoid of lawfulness by mandate of the very Constitution it sought to change which in its Article 31 states;

> ...the acts of anyone who usurps the functions that are not their purview, as well as any act that alleges jurisdiction or applicability not stemming from the law, are null and void.

When we compare the texts of the law for the need to amend with the law for constitutional change we see further proof of the crimes committed and the absolutely devoid nature of it. The proposed text for the law for constitutional change reads;

> Art. 232 The Constitutional Change shall be approved by a simple majority of favorable valid votes cast in the Constitutional Referendum and shall be passed to the Executive for its promulgation and the President of the Republic may not modify it or veto it". The approved text, however, of this same law reads; "Article 232 The total change of the Republic of Bolivia`s Constitution is solely the responsibility of the Constituent Assembly which shall be convened by a Special Convening Law and this assembly will ordain the manner and methods of electing its membership, and shall be approved by two-thirds of votes of those Congressmen present and may not be modified or vetoed by the President of the Republic.

This way the trap was set and Evo Morales, as one of the first things he did after he was sworn in, was to promulgate Law 3464 on 6 March of 2006 convening a "Constituent Assembly" on the basis of the illegally changed text of the Law for Constitutional Change of 20 February of 2004. The new law to convene the Constituent Assembly has mandates that were also violated, for example; Article 6 sets the city of Sucre –the capital city of the Republic- as the site for its meetings, however it was moved into a military garrison and after Evo Morales` ordered massacre at "La Calancha" the Assembly ended up in the city of Oruro; its Article 24 established the period of time for which it would be convened as "a period of uninterrupted and continuous sessions to be of no less than six months and no more than one calendar year after it is convened", however, after one year of being in session it had not approved anything and therefore it no longer (not that it ever did) had the legal competence to continue, but they did; its Article 25 mandated "the Constituent Assembly shall approve the text of the New Constitution with two-thirds of votes…", however, the text of the New Constitution ended up being drafted clandestinely and approved by Congress ignoring the legal mandates for the Constituent Assembly. And if like adding salt to injury, as if the crimes committed up to this point were not enough, Law 3941 was approved and promulgated by Evo Morales on 21 October of 2008 "interpreting" Article 232 (already supplanted in the law for Constitutional Change of 2004) adding to it the following text:

> Upon the conclusion of the Constituent process and following the receipt of its constitutional proposal to be presented for the consideration of the sovereign

people, the Honorable National Congress may modify it, as needed, on the basis of the popular mandate and of national interests, by a Special Congressional Law, approved by two thirds of votes of its members present...

Having done this "they adjusted the constitution to their need" and along with political persecutions, massacres at La Calancha, El Porvenir, Las Americas hotel, Cochabamba and others, and incarcerations, political exiles, and rampant fraud, approved their "Constitution in the mold of the Castroist-Chavoist model" thus creating the "Plurinational State of Bolivia" supplanting the Republic of Bolivia, seeking to divide the "Bolivian nation", promoting rivalry between indigenous nationalities to multiply confrontations between Bolivians, suppressing democratic institutions, and taking the total and indefinite control of power and restructuring everything in their new dictatorial order that now-a-days is labeled as a narco-state.

Currently, in Bolivia, the Castroist-Chavist apparatus manipulates its system "to enable the Chieftain Evo Morales" to take advantage of a despicable Judicial branch, preparing further electoral fraud to keep him in power to assure his impunity, to minimize the economic crisis, cover up the crimes, corruption, and the narco-state. Just like in Venezuela, Cuba, Nicaragua ... but their Constitution is null and void, their governmental acts are criminal and the Bolivian people know it.

OF STUBBORN HISTORY AND TECTONIC FAULT LINES: LEARNING FROM HISTORY TO REBUILD VENEZUELA

Beatrice E. Rangel

I. Introduction

238 years after the creation of Venezuela the world, once again, holds its breath awaiting yet another economic collapse cum bloodshed in the Caribbean country. Many hail the current state of affairs as the triggering factor of a more perfect country capable of delivering on the promise of establishing

> ...a democratic, participatory and self-reliant, multiethnic and multicultural society in a just, federal and decentralized State that embodies the values of freedom, independence, peace, solidarity, the common good, the nation's territorial integrity, comity and the rule of law for this and future generations*.

For knowledgeable historians, however, Venezuela's current predicament is a repetition of the country's many

---

* Preamble Constitution Bolivarian republic of Venezuela

instances into which a world economic turn triggered the fall of a given political order. Accordingly, the looming collapse will give rise to yet another cycle of fictitious political harmony and unsustainable economic progress. Understanding the springs of this predicament becomes fundamental to the task of devising a plan that addresses the fault lines and fosters the development of a more resilient institutional framework that can grow with the country's social and economic development. Lest, of course, Venezuelans and the Hemispheric Community prefer to rebuild the nation on top of a fault line with the express desire of seeing it crumble under the weight of the next world economic shift.

II. A Roller Coaster approach to development?

A cursory review of Venezuela's history reveals a track record of political explosions that led to economic collapse every time that the Atlantic Economy took a turn that bore a direct impact upon the country's terms of trade.

1. Bloody Pearls:

This was the case with pearl exploitation initiated by Christopher Columbus himself and collapsing in 1545 with the fall of New Cadiz the city established in the Cubagua Island. The fall of New Cadiz was preceded by over exploitation and destruction of the oyster beds; internecine fighting between the locals and the Spanish settlers and between their descendants and; the participation of local elites in a conspiracy to open the doors of government to Lope de Aguirre nicknamed The Tyrant. Once in power

Aguirre sacked; mob and killed about 3% of the population depending on how you count the casualties.

> IWn 1561 he seized Margarita Island and held it in a grip of terror. He then crossed to the mainland in an attempt to take Panama, openly proclaiming rebellion against the Spanish crown. Surrounded at Barquisimeto, Venezuela, Aguirre in desperation crowned his infamous life by the murder of his own daughter. He surrendered and was shot*.

According to Simon Velazquez:

> In the early sixteenth century, as today, future hinged on the promise of a particular commodity and the problems associated with its exploitation. It was pearls, not oil or precious metals that first drew Spanish attention to this section of the South American coastline. Treasure hunters initially traded for pearls with indigenous residents of the coast and adjacent islands of Margarita and Cubagua...When relations with the locals soured, Spaniards cast their net wider, enslaving people from the Bahamas to Brazil**.

Over fishing led to reduced production and that to infighting among the different sections of the elite including the descendants of the Guaiquery rulers. After a decade of destructive behavior, Mother Nature decided to inter-

---

* Jose Oviedo y Banos the Conquest and Settlement of Venezuela ; Translation And Annotation by Jeanette Johnson Varner

** Cubagua Ablaze (J. Simón Velásquez 1956:50).

vene and a Caribbean Tsunami wiped New Cadiz away in 1530. According to James Lander and Lowell Whiteside of the University of Colorado in Boulder;

> Sea rose 7.3 m and sank again near coast of Paria and at Cumana and near Island of Cubagua. Ground opened emitting black salt water and asphalt. Mountain at the side of the Gulf of Cariaco was cleft (earthquake). A fort and many houses destroyed, but not clear whether due to the wave, the earthquake or both.

2. A Gift from the Aztecs

Cocoa production which was the next source of development and world recognition for Venezuela followed a similar pattern. The Spaniards fostered the development of cocoa production in Venezuela as reserves of slave labor dwindled in Mexico.

The major cacao producing areas in Mesoamerica, most notably Soconusco, faced a decline in production due to labor shortages at a time when demand was increasing at an enormous rate. Thus, Spain began looking for new places to build cacao plantations. Due to the particular conditions necessary for a cacao plantation to thrive, there were only two choices in New Spain outside of Mexico: Guayaquil in Ecuador and Venezuela. Guayaquil produced the lower quality, cheaper *forastero* variety while Venezuela produced the more desired *criollo* variety. By the middle of the 17th century,

Venezuela had overtaken Mexico as the world's leading producer of cacao. Venezuela went from being a neglected land to one of the most important in New Spain.*

* Laura Kim; Cacao: Impetus for the Creation of an Independent Venezuela

But, alas, the cocoa riches were not to last. Instead of focusing on becoming the unquestionable source of chocolate production for a glutton world, Venezuelan cocoa producers chose to buy real estate in Paris; Madrid and London, to engage in exuberant consumption and to contraband with the Dutch so as to escape ruinous Spanish Crown taxation. The Crowns response did not wait; by 1728 Phillip V granted a monopoly charter over cocoa trade to the Guipuzcoana Company called by most the Caracas Company in light of its unpronounceable name.

This charter set the tune for future oil concessions. Cocoa production started its unstoppable march towards decay. From 65, 000TN production dropped to 43,000 TN over 50 years. By the time of the Independence War cocoa production was decimated.

3. The subjugating aroma of coffee

The next spring of wellbeing was coffee. And although its reign did not last as long as that of cocoa, the approach taken to coffee production did not greatly differ from that of its ancestor commodity. By 1830 Venezuela was the third largest coffee exporter in the world. At this point in time the country was politically polarized. Mr Bolivar had died in exile barred from political participation. The ruling elite were staging yet another economically driven feud.

When the price of coffee fell in the late 1830s and early 1840s, many elite agriculturalists found themselves in serious financial difficulties. Having taken short-term commercial loans at very high interest rates to expand their coffee plantations, the falling export price left them unable to pay interest or principal on these annual or semiannual loans. This situation divided the Venezuelan political elite between planter and merchant interests…This controversy and the subsequent political readjustments saw a transition of government control from one elite group known as the Conservative Oligarchy to another elite group known as the Liberal Oligarchy.*

Bitter disagreement among elite factions opened an opportunity to crown loyalists who found in Jose Tomas Boves the most effective leader. Mr. Boves managed to attract the large population of 'have-nots' inflicting severe defeats to Bolivar and his followers.

José Tomás Rodríguez Boves was a Spanish smuggler and colonist who became a leader of a powerful army during Latin America's struggle for Independence from Spain. Boves' savage horsemen, drawn from the hardy folk who lived on the harsh Venezuelan plains, were known as the "Legion of Hell." He fought for the Spanish against such leaders as Simon Bolívar and Manuel Piar, but answered to no Spanish officer and often acted in his own best interests. Boves was a charismatic leader but also a very cruel and violent man who became known for unspeakable atrocities in the early part of the war.**

---

* John V. Lombardi; The Invention of Venezuela within the World System: The Century of Transition 1750-1850; Jose Gil Fortoul Conference; History Academy of Venezuela, 2000

** Christopher Minster; "Taita Boves: a biography opf Jose Tomas Boves

Boves' led violence was responsible for the death of about 14,000 persons. The population of Venezuela at the time was 718,000 persons

Independence from Spain deepened the divide and soon the country embarked on a destructive Civil War.

Absent a rule of law or an institutional infrastructure higher in authority than the parties in conflict during independence, violence became the ultimate human arbiter*.

The unquestionable leader of this epopee was Ezequiel Zamora who like Boves before him rallied the 'have-nots' to fight what he dubbed as the Goth society. Zamora was an able military leaders and a charismatic politician. Many historians have recorded Mr Zamora's penchant to violence. Over 20,000 died during the Civil War.

4. That goofy substance!!

The oil story follows the same pattern as that of pearls; cocoa and coffee. Venezuela began producing oil in 1878 from a small field near Lake Maracaibo. Commercial production however had to wait until 1914, when the Zumaque well was discovered on the eastern edge of Lake Maracaibo. By World War II Venezuela was the world's largest exporter of oil. The country's oil became a strategic asset for the war effort. During the war, Venezuela passed the Hydrocarbons Law of 1943. This guaranteed the government higher participation in the business, including an increase in domestic refining, and a 16.6 percent royalty in

---

* Ibidem.

exchange for allowing the world's biggest oil companies access to Venezuela's vast reserves for an additional 40 years. The golden era of Venezuelan exploration ensued.

During 1947-60, about 197 new fields were discovered. Production surged from 800,000 barrels per day in 1944 to 3.2 million barrels by 1960. Five new refineries and a gas pipeline to the country's capital began operating. Venezuela solidified its position on the world's stage by helping to launch the Organization of the Petroleum Exporting Countries.

In 1958 the Venezuelan military finally withdrew from national politics. Quality of life improved significantly and the nation flourished. But by the end of the 1970s, a fast, uncontrollable deterioration of the system had begun, and the political-partisan model wore out without any serious attempt to restore the people's confidence. The oil industry was nationalized in 1974 in a climate of internal and external beatitude.

Domestic interests rallied behind the flag seeing great opportunities for expansion in the coming years. Externally concessionaries received a generous payback and the opportunity to participate in future joint ventures with PDVSA. The oil corporate structure remained the same.

Private concessionaries were renamed and were instructed to compete among themselves. All were placed under the holding umbrella company PDVSA. Two and a half decades after PDVSA was created, its proven oil reserves had increased by 420 percent and its natural gas reserves by 360 percent. In the Orinoco Belt, contingent reserves and resources totaled some 250 billion barrels of crude oil and 14.3 billion tons of natural bitumen. The company's equity increased to 8 trillion Bolivars.[*]

PDVSA's subsidiary Intevep became a state of the arts research center with hundreds of patents for instruments, substances, and equipment developed or transformed in its laboratories, and used domestically and worldwide. Internationalization began in 1983. In 1991 at the request of the Ministry of Energy and Mines, PDVSA launched what was deemed to be the beginning of a serious privatization effort. The so called Apertura allowed PDVSA to form operating agreements for the reactivation of marginal fields. It also allowed the creation of petrochemical ventures.

From 1987 these policies triggered the construction of 13 new plants. By 1999, PDVSA held ownership stakes in refineries in Germany, Belgium, the United Kingdom, Sweden, and the United States. At this point in time the institutional edifice was about to succumb once again. The unsolved riddle of how to increase wellbeing without disturbing oil rent extraction was at the root of widespread discontent. Too many believed it possible to continue to extract rent and to jump into the waters of a competitive world economy. This competing visions and ancillary interests created tensions among elite fractions that percolated to the already discontent masses.

Unresponsive demands to the Perez Administration to increase public expenditure created bitterness between political parties and the government, unions and the business community. Most Venezuelans began to distance themselves from democratic means in the belief that the system needed a clean-up exercise. Corruption scandals

---

[*] Gregory Wilpert. *The Economics; Politics And Culture Of Oil In Venezuela.*

rendered this belief stronger. Many began to entertain the idea that an outsider could lead the country to the road of salvation.

Retired lieutenant colonel Hugo Chavez won the presidential election in 1998 based on a populist, anti-neoliberal program and in alliance with governments which rejected the West. He had attempted twice before to enter power through violent means in 1992. He surrendered; went to jail and was pardoned before the trial ended by President Rafael Caldera. He took power without any real opposition from the political establishment. In a very effective manner the Chavez regime called a constitutional assembly followed by a unicameral parliament, imposing the election of pro- government individuals in the national powers, the Supreme Tribunal,

People's Ombudsman, and the General Comptroller's Office. In 2001 a new Hydrocarbons Law was enacted increasing the opportunities to participate in the oil business for the private sector. The law allowed minor reductions in the royalty (fixed at 30 percent) and established a government control of over 50 percent of stock capital in newly formed joint ventures. By its third year, the Chavez government had lost a large part of its initial spontaneous popular support. On December 2, 2002, a strike broke out in opposition to the government. Chavez took advantage of the situation to obtain total control over PDVSA, which was to be managed "by the people and for the people." The fate of the oil industry was sealed. By 2014 PDVSA earnings were about US 32.5B; expenditures surpassed US 40B and; outstanding debt stood at about US 80B.

III. The Twisted Twig of Value Creation

Venezuela's history is one of flip-flopping from growth and stability to poverty and violence. And while other nations in Latin America have shared in this experience, none have had to endure them eternally or with the regularity of a product cycle. This leads us to believe that development of statehood and national identity in Venezuela missed the construction of a national project. In absence of a national project the country continued to operate the economy with the colonial mercantilist apparatus while developing an infrastructure to deal with the rest of the world that bore little or no relation to this apparatus.

This duality serves the purpose of tying together albeit in a loose manner diverse interests during the expansion phase of the development cycle but tends to explode during the restrictive periods of the cycle when losers take it against winners. Stress also builds when major world economic shifts take place, as,

> ...in the early stages of a change, nations may not recognize the nature of the new rules. Internal interests may resist a change that, while optimal for the nation at large, is certain to harm some traditional and politically powerful subgroup*.

This unresolved dilemma has haunted the country for several centuries constraining the development of rule of law and of an institutional framework capable of aggregating interests and resolving conflicts. This also holds at ransom the development of the nation's economic

---

* Lombardi Ibidem

potential given that it nurtures the extractive economic infrastructure while perpetuating the Bolivarian myth and the right of the state to act as economic agent. Should the future leaders of Venezuela fail to remove these obstacles to national formation and economic development; the country will be doomed to experience booms and busts forever.

A. *It's the Economy Stupid*

Venezuela's economic history is one of perpetual extraction as opposed to value creation. Commodities of every sort have been at the heart of economic growth in the country. It all started with pearls followed by cocoa; followed by coffee; followed by oil. And while oil is the only non renewable resource the approach taken to exploitation of pearls; cocoa and coffee followed the logics of an extractive economy rather than those of a value creating economy.

Accordingly, there is no long term vision; no sustained effort to build reserves for the down turns of economic cycles and no valorization of education as the driving force of competitiveness. This short- sightness is the consequence of placing economic initiative in the hands of the state. To break this cycle Venezuela will need to give up public ownership in natural resources. This will remove the greatest obstacle to development: the surviving colonial extractive apparatus that impairs value creation.

B. *Bolivar and the XVIII Brummaire*

Like Marx, Bolivar can be read in so many ways that in the absence of a clear definition of the development path, 18th century Venezuelans chose Bolivar as the incarnation of the national myth given that there were so many readings of his political thinking that there was no need to quarrel or choose. Bolivar further represented the uneasy accommodation reached in Venezuela by 18th century elites between the world economy and local production of export commodities. Like Bolivar the former thrived on the projection of an image of modernity while unfolding a conservative behavior. Or as Lombardi puts it:

> On one side, Venezuela's elite presented a modernizing face to the rapidly expanding, industrializing market economies of the North Atlantic that represented the only source of capital and price-competitive consumer goods and the only market for Venezuela's agricultural export crops.....On the other side, Venezuela's elite managed an internal agricultural production system inherited in all its major characteristics from the clearly no longer competitive Spanish imperial enterprise.

The Bolivarian myth prevented rulers from taking clear cut stands *vis-a-vis* public policies. Thus the cycles of romance and frustration with political leaders that presented one face as campaigners and quite another as rulers.

Putting to rest the Bolivarian myth is yet another foundational task for 21st century Venezuela.

C. Phillip II and his legacy

In spite of retired Lieutenant Colonel Hugo Chavez' strenuous attempts to create a new institutional edifice for Venezuela he left Phillip II legacy intact. At most what Venezuela now has is a medieval building with ArtDeco drapes. The king of Spain that built the Cartagena wall and ordered the preparation of "relaciones geograficas" which were carefully devised census of the American possessions was severely restrained in his powers in Spain and Europe. In the Old Continent dynastic relations and geopolitics established limits to absolute monarchs. Phillip thus set his sight to other more promising horizons. And he created for Spanish America the most fabulous web of regulations ever to rule any territory. And while his representatives would receive the newly enacted royal decrees, placed them next to their right temple and solemnly declare "Accepted but not for execution", their descendants discovered the economic properties of this regulatory wall. Regulations serve the purpose of protecting locals against the disease of competition that is so widespread among those that thrive on international trade. Management of the regulatory wall is a good substitute for rule of law and a bonus payment for bureaucrats. This explains its capacity to survive its creator. For too long a time economic agents in Spanish America have been under the protection of Phillips legacy. And while this continues there will be no competitiveness; transparency or sound management of public goods. Time has come to put Phillip's legacy to rest in Venezuela.

WHY DEMOCRACY IS NOT A CHOICE BUT A NECESSITY

By Luis Fleischman[*]

In the last two decades of this millennium left-wing governments dominated Latin American politics. Some governments respected democracy and democratic transition, such as Brazil, Uruguay, and Chile. Others had full contempt for democracy and sought to abolish it, or important aspects of it, mainly Venezuela and the main countries of the Bolivarian Alliance or ALBA.

However, Latin American countries, through organizations such as the Organizations of American States (OAS) and others, have enabled violations of democracy. The OAS charter spells out what democracy entails and how it should be defended when it is under threat. It embodied the commitment of the countries of the region to implement and guard democracy by generating international pressure on the country that violates democracy, either politically (through isolation) or economically (through sanctions). However, the pretext used by Latin American leaders for ignoring the assault on democracy is the apparent contradiction between the principle of natio-

---

[*] Writer, editor, professor of sociology and political science

nal sovereignty and the OAS Inter-American Democratic Charter.

This article intends to explain that the defense of democracy is important, not only because it offers a more benevolent regime than a dictatorship, but because it represents an important and necessary component of domestic and regional stability.

In this essay, I will explain how Democracy is a mechanism that in modern societies, including most Latin American countries, incorporates civil society so building the rule of law and the state structure. By the same token, I will elucidate how this element of internal stability is likely to benefit the stability and security of the region. Likewise, I will argue that under current circumstances in Latin America, democracy becomes an imperative necessity.

Democracy and Internal Stability

Democracy has different aspects. It is a system of free elections where elites or political parties compete for power. Likewise, democracy enables free development and fosters respect for human, individual, and civil rights to protect citizens from state abuse. However, democracy is also an organizing principle that provides order in societies composed of diverse groups and individuals with different needs, interests, and ideologies.

Democracy is the only regime that recognizes the rights of individuals. Through political rights, it provides a voice to different needs, including material and ideal interests. Political parties, trade unions, business association, social movements, women's groups, environmentalists and others, constitute a political society that organizes to effectively respond to needs generated in civil society. Politics mediates between civil society and the state. Thus, the enacted laws and policies of the state are the direct outcome of civil society's inputs, which include ideal and material compromises. Even though some groups may not be content with specific policies or laws of the states, it is the very democratic procedure and the fair game of democracy that makes these policies and laws legitimate. Legitimacy increases the further the state and its laws represent the outcome of needs generated in civil society. This process also constitutes the foundation of a modern social order.

Many Latin American countries to different degrees have failed to consolidate an order. Two illustrative examples are Venezuela and Ecuador, where the failure to properly integrate civil society, political society, and the state did not provide a lawful modern order. This failure oftentimes culminated in the rise of undemocratic populism and military dictatorship to power.

Since 1958 Venezuela has been mostly governed by two major parties: Accion Democratica (AD) and Comite de Organización Política Electoral Independiente (COPEI). For a long time, both parties shared approximately 80% of the legislative vote and 90% of the presidential vote. Through an agreement known as the "Pact of Punto Fijo", both parties agreed to consult with one another whenever controversial issues arose. Both party leaders seriously tried to avoid conflict since they saw it as a potential threat to their power. Political stagnation plus executive-legislative impasse, were viewed as obstacles to the exercise of governance and a threat to their rule. The parties sought a strong consensus, but this was a consensus of elites with little societal input.

The Punto Fijo pact prevailed for such a long time because it directly related to the production of oil and the use of state resources. The armed forces were remunerated with high salaries, promotions and expensive equipment. Business associations, like Fedecameras consecomercio (commercial council) and conindustria (confederation of industry), were provided with subsidies, low taxes, and protectionist tariffs. Worker unions were rewarded with high salaries as well.

Party discipline and clientelism created a situation similar to a one-party system. These parties created a welfare system based on redistribution and patronage largely sustained by oil revenue. Thus, Venezuelan democracy relied mainly on industrial peace. At the same time, the rigidity of the party came at the expense of the development of autonomous groups within civil society. These two parties attempted to penetrate and exercise influence over most independent organizations like unions and professional associations. These bodies' internal elections were conveyed on the basis of party competition.

The monopolization of political power by this two-party/one party formula inevitably led to rampant corruption, which was further encouraged by a secret clause in the Punto Fijo agreement that prohibited prosecution of corruption.

As long as the two main parties, AD and COPEI, were able to apply redistributionist policies using high price oil revenues, they were also able to maintain the status-quo and keep formal democracy alive. When economic crisis required economic adjustment policies, public discontent caused riots. Slowly the old two-party regime collapsed.

At the time of Chavez's election, the two dominant political parties were regarded as corrupt entities that squandered the country's vast oil wealth and left a tremendous gap between rich and poor. Thus, Hugo Chavez emerges in the election of 1998 as an elected "Bonapartist" figure, against the background of a severe conflict and party crisis. The concept of "Partidocracia" or oligarchical rule by the parties, was a slogan used by Hugo Chavez and others to de-legitimize the old regime. This type of discourse against the two-party establishment and the adjustment measures helped him win the elections in 1998.

In Ecuador, after a 10-year dictatorship (1969-1979), the constitutional order was finally restored. As democracy was reinstated, a strong indigenous movement embodied in the Confederación de Nacionalidades Indigenas del Ecuador (CONAIE) emerged. This organization represented 40% of the Indian population, which began to surface from Ecuador's political marginality. Parties in Ecuador became vehicles to empower a political leadership of elites, but they failed to incorporate social movements and new groups into the system. Leadership continued to use elections simply as vehicles to be elected. Change of ideology for personal gain was a very common phenomenon among members of the political class. As an example, one-third of those elected to Congress in 1992 had switched parties because the other party made promises of government patronage. This detachment undermined the possibility of building mass constituencies and thus weakened the system's ability to incorporate social groups.

The indigenous community was the most excluded and no party reached out to them. The Indigenous population began street demonstrations and pressed cultural recognition, bi-lingual education, and land reform-demands but to no avail. These protests were occasionally met with repressive measures. Indigenous and popular resentment increased.

In 1996 Ecuadorians elected an "outsider" as President of Ecuador, Abdala Bucaram, who capitalized on Ecuadorians' general discontent. A poll conducted in 1996 indicated that 64% of Ecuadorians preferred dictatorship over democracy and that the armed forces and the Catholic Church were the most respected institutions. Bucaram carried out economic adjustment measures, which included higher taxes and tariffs. These policies plus increasing government corruption raised the rage of the middle classes and the increasingly powerful indigenous movement. Stoppages and strikes forced Bucaram out of power.

Instead of enlarging representation, traditional parties proceeded to carry out a constitutional reform aimed at strengthening the executive power. Latin America's decision to neglect parliament has been one of its most significant problems. It has always sought to solve problems by having a powerful executive branch at the expense of parliament, which is the arena where compromises and public debate take place. Ecuador's new constitution took away power from parliament without solving any problems.

In 1998 a new President and the former Mayor of Quito, Jamil Mahuad, was elected. As oil prices fell in the international market, an economic downfall took place. Mahuad announced the takeover of people's deposits and a new policy of dollarization. The decision was made overnight with little public debate. Soon after, indigenous organizations marched in the streets in masses demanding a change in economic policy and Mahuad's resignation. The military supported the movement, creating a military Junta for the sake of national salvation. Lucio Gutierrez led this military initiative and established ties to the indigenous movements. After Mahuad's resignation, Gutierrez ran in national elections as an outsider and won.

However, once in power, Gutierrez moved to adopt economic austerity policies contrary to the populist redistributionist policies he voiced in his electoral campaign. These policies brought the indigenous movement's immediate withdrawal of support. As discontent grew, political repression increased and Gutierrez' cronies replaced members of the Supreme Court.

Further street uprisings followed, where the demonstrators called to expel the political class. The demonstrators' slogan "Que se Vayan Todos" (Let them all go home) echoed a chant already heard a year and a half earlier in Argentina, where street demonstrators expressed their distrust for the political class and the political system. Congress finally removed Gutierrez in the aftermath of massive demonstrations dominated by distrustful indigenous people. Gutierrez' removal paved the way for the rise of Rafael Correa, who, like Chavez, ran on a strong anti-establishment platform.

Deception before elections is not unusual in Latin American political culture. Candidates make promises during the electoral campaign, and once they are in power they feel entitled to govern without honoring them. Scholar Guillermo O'Donnell has called this practice "Delegative Democracy." According to "Delegative Democracy," "whoever wins election to the presidency is thereby entitled to govern as he or she sees fit. " The President is taken to be the embodiment of the nation and the chief custodian and definer of its interests. However, "Delegative Democracy" works only as long as the population remains passive or as long as economic bonanza conceals these institutional deficiencies.

When parties do not respond directly to constituencies; when political leaders believe that the act of voting is an automatic mandate that does not require further consultations with elements in civil society, alienation and detachment between civil society and elected officials take place. In Ecuador and Venezuela, as we have seen, parties did not properly represent civil society. Parties and political leaders stood as supreme entities empowered only by the act of voting.

Such estrangement enables a situation where society cannot advance its diverse concerns, and at the same time, the state and the political elite remain unaccountable and corrupt. In this scenario, the whole democratic regime suffers a crisis of legitimacy.

The challenge is therefore to promote a sound democracy. On the one hand, this democracy should be based on freedom and pluralism. On the other hand, it is crucial to institute a strong state, capable of absorbing the different needs and inputs from the shifts in civil society and establish a legitimate democratic relationship with civil society. This style of democracy is important not only to maintain the legitimacy of the democratic regime but also to strengthen the rule of law and the state capacity to govern.

On the Importance of Democracy, Legality, and Governability

It is important to differentiate between a democratic regime and a democratic state. Electoral politics mainly characterize democratic systems. They hold regular and fair elections and conduct regular presidential or other offices' transitions. All citizens have the right to vote and be elected. By the same token, there is an element of freedom of expression and freedom of association. In this sense, the majority of Latin American countries can be defined as democratic regimes. However, a democratic state includes all of the above but also a strong legal system and state structure that backs the rights and freedoms that exist in a democratic regime. A democratic state must contain an adequate legal system where actors such as judges can act independently and professionally to follow a fair procedure and not a political order.

Laws must be designed with the input and participation of civil society, since the institutional and legal framework of the state must be designed by and for the people. By civil society, we mean the inclusion of individuals, movements, interest groups, trade unions, religious groups, and associations of all kinds that seek to advance their interests whether they are material or ideal, whether they seek new labor policies, corporate advantages, the advancement of women's rights or any other issue. Enacted laws must be the result of compromises and exchange of ideas in civil society that take place in parliament. Likewise, the laws, those who enforce them and those who regulate them, must become part of the institutional setting of the state. This is the real rule of law and the foundation of a robust state democracy. This is a more perfected version of what Max Weber would call a rational-legal state, a state whose laws are obeyed because of its legitimate foundation. By the same token, as Hannah Arendt pointed out, the division of powers that includes a strong legislative power and an independent judiciary are generators of social power. Democracy enables social power and at the same constitutes a method through which this power is organized. Thus, if this process is successful, it creates a state structure that becomes the backbone of order.

Thus, a democratic state can govern better and more efficiently than a state that is authoritarian or a government that ignores republican procedure or the division of powers altogether. Furthermore, as the state and its laws emanate from civil society, people are more likely to respect the laws and policies of the state. No less important, the administrative structure created is more likely to facilitate the state's ability to govern precisely because is the result of a process that originates in civil society. Last but not least, well-enforced laws can create an environment of legality and stability that could prevent powerful economic groups, dictators, drug traffickers or all of the above from colonizing the state.

In Latin America, we have witnessed the emergence of democracies that take place in weak states. One of Latin America's fundamental problems is that the executive power has overrun the legislature and the judiciary.

According to a OAS report, in Latin America half of the 18 presidents have assumed functions usually designated to members of Parliament or the legislative brunch. According to this report, the weakness of Republicanism is the result of an exacerbated Presidentialism and often rule by decree.

If a legitimate rational-legal democratic state fails, we are likely to continue to see angry masses appealing to charismatic leaders. These leaders are seen as sources of hope and order. One could suggest this is what enabled Chávez, Correa, and Morales to re-found the state altogether. In those cases, authoritarian charisma and messianic hope replaced the absence of a strong legitimate law and institutional setting. Furthermore, when the state and its laws are weak even if they do not succumb to a populist dictatorship, they may well succumb to the dominance of drug cartels that take advantage of corruption and poor economic conditions. Countries in Central America represent clear examples of this.

It is against this background that we can understand the importance of democracy in the international context.

Democracy in the International Context

Weak states can produce populist dictators and revolutionary situations such as in Venezuela and the ALBA countries. The impunity and sense of power experienced by a populist dictator leads him to exercise arbitrary rule without accountability. This sense of entitlement could lead the ruler to engage in dangerous activities such as connections with rogue states, drug cartels, and terrorist groups. Such activities can endanger the entire region. This happened with Hugo Chavez who not only engaged in dangerous activities in Venezuela but also "evangelized" these policies among like-minded rulers in the region. By the same token, Chavez' impunity has made Venezuela into a narco-state that is now jeopardizing the region.

Similarly, in Central America, weak democratic and legally enfeebled states have created de-facto anarchical narco-states. In Guatemala, drug cartels have taken over almost every aspect of life and have dragged the state personnel with them through the corruption of public and law enforcement officials. Mexico has become an area of carnage without precedent. Drug money has become an important source of funding for Islamist terrorists. The expansion of such anarchy, like the expansion of ruthless dictatorships, constitutes a geo-political threat to the region.

Therefore, it is in the interests of the countries of the region to help strengthen all the mechanisms that enforce the power of the legal state because such advance of criminal organizations has become a threat to them all.

Also, the more countries practice democracy, the more likely it is that they will share values of freedom and tolerance. Those values will make a democratic state reject alliance with rogue states, terrorist groups, and drug cartels, which is what Venezuela and some of its allies in the region are doing.

Currently, these problems are exacerbated by the multiplication of elected authoritarian rulers who follow rogue behavior. Venezuela is a narco-state that has strengthened relations with Iran and terrorist organizations.

Real democratic states do not willingly become narco-states as Venezuela has. Strong democratic-legal states do not become colonized by drug cartels as Mexico and certain countries in Latin America have.

Conclusion

To conclude, the OAS Democratic Charter has been viewed as interfering with national sovereignty, but national sovereignty means a strong legal state that is built on democracy. And legal states mean a more stable and safe region. National sovereignty cannot become the principle that protects a usurper of societal power or his right to destroy a much needed legality. Democracy is not a choice but a necessity and therefore it is the obligation of OAS members to fight for it and strengthen it.

PANDORA'S BOX -2017-

The future has many names.
For the weak is the unreachable.
For the fearful, the unknown.
For the, brave the opportunity.
Victor Hugo

By César Vidal[*]

At the start of this New Year, I have to withdraw from the habit of writing on a particular subject. To review in this Pandora the countries in which, in my opinion, the events that will happen and will define the course of the new year, Which will undoubtedly be appreciated and evaluated in a different way —as the author of "Les Miserables" tells us— for the weak, the fearful and the brave.

The 2017 dawn with certain possibilities of occurrence of regional conflicts that will contribute to draw the global panorama that we will face in the months to come. With that in mind, I will then refer to the geographical areas that I think we should observe in order to have an overview that reasonably allows us to predict what we will face in the next 12 months:

---

[*] Historian, writer and communicator.

America

Argentina and Brazil. Both South American giants face very similar problems, since their respective governments do not have a solid popular support due, in the Argentine case, to the narrow margin of victory obtained by Mauricio Macri in the last presidential elections and, in the case of Brazil, For the character of interinato that has the government of Michel Temer as a consequence of the impeachment of its president. Their economies are also seriously affected by the years of populist policies implemented by the Peronist and PT governments, respectively, implying that both governments should adopt measures of shock that will not be welcomed by the parasite society born under the auspices of Governments of Lula da Silva and Rousseff in Brazil and of the Kirchners in Argentina. Fortunately, in both countries, institutions remain, and this has led to the discovery and prosecution of gigantic cases of corruption that directly affect their political class and especially their top leadership, who have already been charged with economic crimes and corruption. As for the cases of Cristina Kirchner, Petrobras and Odebrecht, many will be the names of Venezuelans who will be identified in the investigations being carried out, which will constitute a volatile ingredient in the mega crisis that is brewing in Venezuela.

Bolivia. At the beginning of 2016, the Bolivian people gave a clear "NO" to Evo Morales' persistent pretensions. Since then, the tenant of the Palacio Quemado looks for a way to obviate the popular decision and run for a third term (a quarter in reality) in the 2019 elections. In Bolivia, internal conflicts can be expected due to the economic downturn caused by the The prices of raw materials exported by Bolivia (oil, gas and zinc), the rise of the dollar against the Bolivian and cases of corruption, influence traffic and abuse of power. In addition, the critical drought situation that affects much of the territory of the highlands can influence the social peace of Bolivians. Nevertheless, the Morales government can take advantage of the dispute with Chile over its departure to the Pacific, to manipulate the people and obtain support for its continuation claim.

Cuba. In his speech to the Assembly of People's Power on December 27, Raul Castro painted a not very flattering picture for the Cuban economy, which suffered a decrease of 0.9% in 2016, which leads to the announced difficulty of Comply with the commitments of international payments, motivated, according to Castro, to a significant reduction in the availability of Cuba's third export product: Venezuelan oil. This negative picture had already been recognized by the economy minister Ricardo Cabrisas, who announced on December 27 that Cuba had entered recession. In any case, in Cuba post Fidel reigns the uncertainty with the ascension to the presidency of Donald Trump from this January 20 and the installation of a Congress of Republican majority. Recall that among the electoral promises made by Trump to the Cuban community in the important state of Florida, is the revision of agreements signed with the Obama administration, especially in economic and financial matters, which could affect the tourist activity of the island (Main source of income), which is basically in the hands of the GAESA holding owned by the Cuban Armed Forces, headed by General Luis Alberto

López-Calleja, Raul Castro's son-in-law. On the other hand, the jet-laundering investigation also seems to reach GAESA due to its relationship with Odebrecht and the Port of Mariel.

Colombia. Our neighbor also has institutional problems, as President Santos has tried to pass over the will of the Colombian people, not submitting to a new popular consultation the definitive agreement negotiated with the FARC. It seems that for all practical purposes the irregulars —including the ELN— have already accepted their demobilization and their incorporation into Colombian institutional life. What is not clear is what will be the final destination of the lucrative drug business that could well be transferred to Venezuelan territory, to border areas controlled by the Colombian facinerosos.

Ecuador. President Correa is not doing well. He already announced that he will not be a candidate in the elections that take place this month of February and recently declared that the Odebrecht scandal possibly sprinkles him. Ecuador's economic situation is not flattering since with the 2.5% drop in GDP in 2016, it is clear that the country has entered a recession. As in Venezuela, the fall in oil prices led to a drastic reduction of social spending, a cornerstone of Correa's populist policies, which, unlike Morales and Maduro, shrewdly decided to leave the game and leave another To face the crisis that is looming, since it will not be a candidate for reelection in the elections of February 2017.

U.S. Since the 1948 election campaign between Truman and Dewey there was no electoral result such as the one that led Donald Trump to the presidency of the United

States, obtaining this a large victory in electoral votes, but losing with Mrs. Clinton in the vote Popular by more than 3 million votes. Trump arrives at the presidency with a clear anti-political and anti-system message that promises to move the foundations of the American establishment. Never before has a US presidential election provoked as much controversy after it was held as Trump has been in the presidency. So we could see it in the violent demonstrations in different cities carried out by opponents of Trump, and in the unveiled efforts of CNN to stimulate the counting of votes in key states. I think it is risky to make predictions about the performance of the new president because one thing is the diatriba of campaign and another very different day to day of the internal and external management of the only power that today subsists. In any case, Trump has given concrete evidence of its close relationship with Israel, which would undoubtedly affect the geopolitics of the Middle East; Nor has it concealed its intention to approach Russia strategically in order to separate it from China (in contrast to Nixon's strategy in 1972) and has manifested its declared economic isolationism, the first evidence of which we appreciate in the threat of the president-elect of To punish the Ford Motor Company for its intention to install an assembly plant (maquila) in Mexico. Those who know about American politics say that the most precious gem of the American presidency is to be able to shape the nation's judiciary towards presidential thinking. Well, Donald Trump will have that golden opportunity because he has to fill 100 vacancies at the level of the federal judiciary, including that of one of the 9 Associate Judges of the Supreme Court of the United

States, following the death of Judge Antonin Scalia in February 2016. The appointment of the new Associate Judge by the President requires the approval of the Senate (of Republican majority) and whoever is appointed will be the faithful of the balance between liberals and conservatives in the Court, since both factions have 4 Judges each a.

Mexico. The Aztec country has not been a disturbing factor in the Americas since Jose Doroteo Arango Arámbula (a.k.a. Pancho Villa) "invaded" the United States in 1916, attacking the border town of Columbus, New Mexico. I have always thought that the main and most productive asset of Mexico —after its history and folklore— is the Rio Grande, its border with the United States. However, this does not look like this in the future, even before his installation as president, Donald Trump began to raise his promised border wall, which we evidenced with the president-elect's threat to the Ford Motor Company to punish it with taxes if he installed A projected automotive plant in Mexican soil. If the xenophobic threats of the new White House tenant materialized, we could see an instability in Mexico that would benefit the already uncontrolled drug business and that would stimulate a migratory crisis toward the north as has not been seen to date. As if it were a warning of the future, at the beginning of the year looting and public order alterations occurred in Mexico City as a result of a 40% increase in the price of gasoline, which presages a year of no peace for President Peña Grandchild.

Venezuela. On January 5, 2017, the National Assembly was installed with a new Board of Directors headed by Deputy Julio Borges. That same day announced the designation of a new cabinet ministerial headed by the governor of Aragua, Tarek El Aisami, that substitutes an Aristobulus Isturiz that no longer cheers when they discard it like waste. To this date it is obvious that the ill-conceived attempt to dialogue with the government is no more than an exercise in futility, since it served only to shore up the government, to discredit the opposition leadership before public opinion and to expose the treason, Of the mercenary Venezuelan political caste. The social situation that Venezuelans live, due to the hyper-inflation that has already made its formal appearance in the country, insecurity and lack of food and medicines, is certainly explosive as seen last December in several cities, especially in The Bolivar state. To predict that in Venezuela there will be a total breakdown of the social order is not a challenge; But to predict when it will take place is more uphill, for there is in truth no single objective reason for the dreaded anarchy to have already occurred. In any case, 2017 begins with the promise of being definitive for the future of Venezuela because in the coming weeks will have to define the course that will assume the Republic. The confrontation between the National Assembly and the regime is already announced. On the one hand, there is talk of dissolution of the Legislative Branch via a ruling of the Constitutional Chamber and, on the other, of the declaration of abandonment of the position of who today holds the Executive Power. On the government side, there is a clear radicalization evident in recent ministerial appointments. On the side of the Assembly, I have heard statements by its members that the issue of Maduro's nationality (and now that of the new Vice-President) will be resumed; It is intended to appoint the new magistrates of the Supreme Court of Justice, as a result of having revoked on July 14 the last appointment by the outgoing National Assembly on December 23, 2015, and the designation of the 5 rectors of the CNE , Elected illegally by the Constitutional Chamber of the Supreme Court of Justice. Equally premonitory was the statement of Archbishop Jorge Urosa Sabino, who, following the example of his predecessor Monsignor Arias Blanco in the years of the Pérez Jiménez dictatorship, urged his parishioners "to rebel against the dictatorship." Be that as it may, something is clear: Venezuela reached zero hour.

Europe

Germany, France and the Netherlands. In 2017 these three countries representing 40% of the European economy will have elections. In these elections the triumph of parties of the European right is expected which will imply drastic changes in the immigration policy and the permanence of those countries in the European Union. England will activate Article 50 of the Treaty of Lisbon in March 2017, anticipating its departure from the EU for the summer of 2019.

Italy. Europe's third largest economy is on track to cause damage to the Euro and to the very existence of the European Union, even more damaging than Brexit itself. The banking crisis in Italy is about to collapse the payment system of that country, motivated by the inefficiency of credit institutions that accumulate about 360,000 million euros in bad loans. According to European legislation, member states are virtually barred from bailing out their financial institutions, so the Italian government will have to breach European law if it decides to inject public money into distressed banks. In any case, Italy represents another clear danger for the continuity of the European Union and its single currency.

Russia. Vladimir Putin's Russia is a very active player in world geopolitics and we saw this in relation to Ukraine, the Baltic States and, particularly, the conflict in Syria. Putin, raised and trained under the Russian security and espionage system, was director of the Federal Security Service (SFS) —heiress of the Soviet KGB— and is a fervent nationalist and anti-Islamist. The president is very popular in the Russian Federation and has become a kind of pop icon whose image has been collected in the famous matryoshka dolls and in calendars that display images of him in different macho poses like Rambo. Putin knows that Russia is no longer able to challenge the United States in a linear war, so its strategy is aimed at weakening the West with localized actions that seek to recover some of the lost spaces from the disintegration of the Soviet Union in 1991. We have therefore seen its annexation of the Crimean peninsula, its intervention disguised in Eastern Ukraine, the pressure it has subjected to the Baltic States and its military involvement in the Syrian conflict, where Moscow has real strategic interests that focus on its Mediterranean naval base in Tartus, Syria. Let us not forget that, as a consequence of the astonishing destruction suffered by Russia in its territory during World War II, the Russian defensive doctrine during the cold war was to fight the next war in the territory of its Eastern European satellites. This strategic approach today is not possible because literally the Russian Federation has its enemy at home because all countries bordering Russia are members of the Atlantic Alliance, with the exception of Belarus, the only Moscow ally on the north-south axis of its Western border.

Turkey. The country that Tsar Nicholas II called "the sick man of Europe" gave much to speak in 2016. In Turkey there were bloody terrorist attacks, armed clashes with Syrian and Russian forces and a self-evident blow struck by the constituted power , So it is not difficult to predict that that country will be in the eye of the hurricane in 2017. Turkey, the heir of the Ottoman Empire, entered modernity in the twentieth century thanks to the efforts of Mustafa Kamal Ataturk, who created a state Modern, but above all, secular. Today, the Turks are facing their historical enemies, the Kurds and so have allied with Russia and Iran to keep President Bashar Al Assad in power in Syria. This unnatural alliance illustrates the complexity of the political game in the area that could lead to a military attack by Russia or Iran on Turkey, which could lead, according to Article 50 of the North Atlantic Treaty, to NATO participation in Defense of Turkey, a member of that military alliance since 1952. For greater concern, current President Recep Tayyip Erdogan, a Turkish, anti-Armenian and Kurdish nationalist, but a practicing Muslim, hopes to be able to eliminate, by a referendum convened for this 2107, Current parliamentary political system to turn it into a purely presidentialist. In any case, with the arrival of Trump to the White House, who has expressed his unconditional support for Israel and has said that the United States has nothing to look for in the Middle East, we must be aware of serious regional conflicts involving Turkey , Those that could overflow and affect the rest of Europe. As a matter of concern, I point out that, in Germany, the engine of Europe, there are (according to the latest census) 2,700,000 Turks, which undoubtedly represents an Islamic "Trojan Horse" in the heart of Europe.

The Vatican. Pope? And how many divisions does the Pope have? History tells us that Stalin answered his interlocutor, Pierre Laval, at his meeting in Moscow in 1935, when the Frenchman asked for his help to improve his relationship with the Vatican. Indeed the power of the Vatican is not measured in divisions but in thousands of years of experience and its participation in world events has been very active, sometimes with positive results and sometimes not so much, as recently happened in Venezuela. The Holy See played a major role in the US approach. Cuba, thanks to which the United States, in the post-Fidel era, are positioned to influence the future of the island with a view to improving the living conditions of the Cuban people. It seems that the Vatican has also played an important role in the current crisis in the Middle East, especially in Syria, with the intention of protecting the Christians who have lived for millennia in those lands. Recalling what was said by Monsignor Pietro Parolin, Secretary of State of the Holy See in a conversation in Caracas with which he privileged me, we must not forget that Syria was the cradle of the greatest of followers of Jesus: The Apostle St. Paul.

Middle East

Saudi Arabia and Iran. The conflicts that today affect the Islamic countries of the Middle East, started from the death of Muhammad (Muhammad ibn Abdallah) in the year 632 of our era and originated fundamentally motivated to positions found with respect to the succession of the Prophet. When it came to designating Muhammad's successor, umma (the Community of Islam) was divided among those who claimed that the new leadership would fall on someone linked to Muhammad by blood (Shiites) and others who claimed that the heir was someone Which had the same qualities and virtues of the Prophet (Sunnis). That confrontation that led to two civil wars or fitnas in the years 656-660 and 680-692, continues in our days motivated to the continuation of the ancient confrontation between the two main factions of Islam and the unnatural ethnic and territorial partition made by the League Of Nations in 1920 made the allied powers after the First World War of the territories that were part of the failed Ottoman Empire. The countries that now lead and fuel this confrontation are Iran and Saudi Arabia. The Islamic Republic of Iran, overwhelmingly Shiite (the minority sect of Islam), is a non-Arab Persian theocracy that confronts the West, especially the United States (The Great Satan). Recently, the international community reached an agreement by which Iran — supposedly — renounced its nuclear program in exchange for financial concessions, especially the release of its assets held by President Obama's government. However, Iran represents a clear and real danger to the stability of the area as its control of the vital Strait of Hormuz in the Persian Gulf has led to incidents with the United States navy. For its part, the Sunni Kingdom of Saudi Arabia, guardian of the holy sites of Islam, Mecca and Medina, is an Arab monarchy with close Western ties given its character as the main oil producer in the Middle East. Iran and Saudi Arabia have pushed their confrontation across countries and interposed organizations, as evidenced today in Syria, where the Saudi Kingdom supports the Sunni guerrillas fighting against Bashar al-Assad (supported by Russia, Iran and Turkey), while Iran Supports the Houties (Shiite) rebels in predominantly Sunni Yemen. However, with the execution of a Shia cleric by Saudi Arabia in January 2016, the confrontation took on a more direct character as the Saudi embassy was burned in Tehran in retaliation for execution and both countries severed diplomatic relations. We should not presume that there are good and bad guts in this conflict, since what is being discussed is the primacy of one religious sect over the other, within a religious universe that is in essence confronted with Western Judeo-Christian civilization from the time of The second Crusade (1144-1148). So complicated is the framework we see today in the Middle East that in the case of Syria and Iraq we see alliances of opportunity that do not really seek to solve the tragedy of those countries, but impose on the rival sect, with a view to assuming religious control , Political and economic of the umma that the Prophet Muhammad founded. The fact that this eminently religious power conflict between the representatives of the two main sects of Islam has not yet directly confronted them does not mean that at a given juncture the two rivals collide militarily, which would lead other actors to assume positions in the Conflict given the vital importance to the West of the area's main asset: oil.

Iraq. The so-called "Cradle of Civilization" is today a failed state that seeks to restructure itself after the wars that put an end to Saddam Hussein. In Iraq there is also evidence of internal strife motivated by religious differences (Shiites against Sunnis) and the inclusion in their territory of nationalities historically opposed to each other, as is the case of the Kurds who were persecuted by the Saddam government, who used weapons Chemical and biological weapons against the Kurdish civilian population. Baghdad is struggling to take control of its territory today and faces terrorism and the insurgency from the war in Syria, mainly from the so-called Islamic State, which, according to the Western intelligence services, originated from elements of the Ba ' Ath who ruled Iraq until 2003.

Syria. The current conflict in Syria began in early 2011 and shows an amalgam of clashes and alliances that show that what matters least to the participants, is the Syrian people. The Iranians, Russians and Turks support Bashar al-Assad with troops and means of combat, fighting against rebels who are supported by the United States and Saudi Arabia, France and England. There is also presence of the Islamic State that controls a significant part of the Syrian territory. As I pointed out before, everyone has their interests in this war that will ultimately lead to the disintegration of Syria as we know it today. The Russians support the Asad, being their protege from the time of the Soviet Union and maintaining its Mediterranean naval base at Tartus; The Iranians support Baghdad for facing Saudi Arabia that supports the Sunni majority guerrillas and Turkey intervenes to curb their enemies the Kurds.

As we can see, this conflict, where chemical weapons have been used and which has killed more than 450,000 people and caused the displacement of 7.5 million men, women and children, is the most bloody confrontation in the world today. The destruction of entire cities, as was the case with ancient Aleppo, and the atrocities committed by the so-called Islamic State (ISIS) guerrillas. In any case, this conflict seems to increase in intensity with the resent car bomb attacks in Baghdad and Damascus, which have cost dozens of civilian lives. On the other hand, the war is proving costly for those involved, as in the case of Russia that ordered the withdrawal of Syrian water from its aircraft carrier Admiral Kuznetsov. In any case, we must be aware of the confrontation between Iran and Saudi Arabia that can well overflow Syria and end in a linear war between the two countries.

India and Pakistan. It is foreseeable that these historical enemies will continue the border incidents in Kashmir and terrorist incursions in India promoted by the Pakistani intelligence service (ISI). However, I think that the animosity will not overflow to another linear war as happened in 1947, 1965 and 1971, as both countries now have a nuclear arsenal and missiles capable of destroying each other. For this reason the conflicts that happen in the region due to the religious differences between Muslims and Hindus will continue being of low intensity motivated to the application of the same military doctrine that maintained the nuclear peace between the former Soviet Union and the United States during the Cold War : Mutual Destruction Insured or MAD in its acronym in English.

Far East

China. The Asian giant is undoubtedly a force to be taken into account in global geopolitics. China ceased to be a localized power to expand its influence at the global level, supported not by its military might but by its economic strength. In the military, China has projected its navy outside the coastal brown waters to venture into the blue waters, for which it has a carrier, Liaoning, and two more under construction. At present, Beijin is building and militarizing artificial islets in the South China Sea, in the islands of the Paracelsus and Spratly Islands, triggering boundary disputes with Indonesia, Malacia, Brunei, the Philippines and Vietnam. The background of this offshore expansionist policy is to re-establish in the sea the old "Silk Route", the one that would pass through the Venetian Marco Polo in the thirteenth century, in order to have a safe commercial maritime route —the Chinese trade reached In 2015 the combined figure of $ 4.3 trillion— across the China Sea, the Strait of Malacca, the Indian Ocean, Africa, the Middle East and, hence, Europe. In any case, it seems that China's intention is to secure its markets, so it is not likely to seek any confrontation with the West, especially with the United States Navy. However, it would be convenient for China to reassure the waters on the Korean peninsula, lest her protege in Pyongyang involve her in a war that is not in her interest. Finally, we must be aware of what will be the position of Donald Trump with respect to Taiwan that is considered by Beijin as one of its provinces. Any change from the current quocon status with regard to Taiwan involving mainly the United States can become a dangerous confrontation that no one agrees with.

North Korea. If we wanted to imagine an absolutely bizarre, obscurantist country, out of one of those imaginary realms of evil that we fought in violent video games, North Korea would be the undisputed candidate. We speak of a country where its inhabitants die of hunger; Where its leaders (grandfather, son and grandson) are attributed powers over nature, and in which men and women must choose between 12 haircuts previously approved by an official commission of public appearance. In truth, this Kim family inheritance would not deserve even being taken seriously, if not because it possesses not only nuclear capability and the missile means for its use, but it is directed by a "Supreme Leader" who recently executed with an anti-aircraft gun To his defense minister for falling asleep during one of his speeches. We must not forget that the state of war is still in force between the two Koreas and the young Kim Jong-un, in one of his usual outbursts and tantrums, could take advantage of the political instability in Seoul to launch a military attack that would undoubtedly involve Would militarily face China, Japan and the United States.

Philippines. With the signing of the Treaty of Paris of 1899, Spain ceded to the United States Cuba, Puerto Rico, Guam and the Philippines. From the very beginning of the 20th century, the Americans began to have problems with the Filipino insurgents, led by Emilio Aguinaldo. As an anecdotal piece of information I refer to the fact that US troops confronted serious problems when they were attacked by Moorish guerrillas who charged the machete soldiers with their machete soldiers without their (38-gauge semiautomatic) pistols could stop the insurgent charge. This caused the American Army to procure a weapon with greater stopping power, which led to the development of the famed Colt 45 automatic pistol, model ACP 1911, which remained the standard weapon of the armed forces of the United States from 1911 to 1985. Americans maintained the Philippines as a colony and it was only after the Japanese invasion in December 1941 that Washington promised independence to the archipelago in order to gain their support in the fight against the Japanese. The Americans fulfilled their commitment and on July 4, 1946, the Philippines gained full independence. Since then, Manila has been a close ally of the United States, which maintained important air and naval bases in its territory to protect the Southeast Asian zone of potential communist incursions. This strategic alliance, embodied in SEATO (version of NATO in Southeast Asia), has remained until today motivated to the arrival to the power of Rodrigo Duterte who has been dedicated to attack the United States looking for ally with the Chinese and with the Russians Duterte, who will visit Moscow in April this year, said in a recent visit to Russian warships in Manila that the Russians were welcome in the Philippines, including as allies and protectors. It is not risky to speculate that the CIA must already be taking action in the matter, making contact with elements of the Philippine armed forces, who have historically been the arbiters of that country's policy.

Japan. General Douglas MacArthur imposed upon the vanquished Japan a constitution in which not only was the "divine" character attributed to the Emperor, but also prohibited the Japanese Defense Force from entering its territory. Japan is today a first-world nation with a strong and expanding economy. Prime Minister Shinzo Abe has maintained close relations with the United States, especially in the area of security and defense. Japan currently has good relations with its neighbors —of course excluding North Korea— but maintains a border dispute over the Senkaku Islands, disputed with China and Taiwan. Although there is no "lost love" with China and Korea motivated to the atrocities committed by the Japanese army in World War II against the citizens of those countries, a confrontation in the near future that involves Japan is not predictable. However, it is not ruled out that provocations by Chucky of North Korea that alter the stability of the area.

As we can see, the year 2017 promises to be very dynamic and fraught with uncertainty and from the very beginning a geopolitical picture is drawing that is really worrying and not at all encouraging.

Caracas, January 5, 2017

(Translated by Lizandra Garriga)

www.ingramcontent.com/pod-product-compliance
Lightning Source LLC
Chambersburg PA
CBHW050929260726
48660CB00001B/478